SPICE I AM

Sujet Saenkham of Sydney's critically acclaimed Spice I Am restaurant stable was born in a remote village in Central Thailand, where he learnt to cook treasured family recipes at his mother's and grandparents' sides. After switching from an accounting degree to studying science with a major in chemistry in Bangkok, in 1985 Sujet ventured to Australia and loved it so much that he decided to make Sydney his home. Here, he studied hospitality, and his long-held ambition of becoming an executive chef was realised in 2004, when he opened the doors of Spice I Am in Sydney's Surry Hills. This hole-in-the-wall was immediately adopted as the Thai restaurant of choice for the city's food media, and the restaurant empire has since expanded to include a more sophisticated restaurant in Darlinghurst; an offshoot in Balmain; a restaurant called House Thai, which specialises in Issan dishes from the north of Thailand; and, in 2014, Surry Hills Eating House opened, showcasing the regional cuisine of southern Thailand. This is Sujet's first cookbook.

For more information, visit spiceiam.com

SPICE I AM

SUJET SAENKHAM

PHOTOGRAPHY BY
ROB PALMER

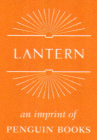

LANTERN

an imprint of
PENGUIN BOOKS

I dedicate this book to my mother,
who is the major inspiration for my cooking

CONTENTS

My mother and younger siblings at a nearby beach, 1980.

My parents, grandparents and siblings
at my sister's wedding, 1996.

My mother and I in front of our chicken farm, 1993.

My younger brother and I when I was in year 12,
with the local school behind us, 1983.

My father, sister and I at our new house, 1993.

INTRODUCTION

GROWING UP IN THAILAND

I was born in 1964 in Nasamor, a small rural village in the Ratchaburi province in central Thailand. Most of the people in my hometown were extended family on my mother's side, and were of Laos ethnic background, speaking Lao and practising Thai-Lao culture. Many of the old-style houses were made from lathed bamboo, although some families had solid teak houses. My family was poor, but my father had worked in logging when he was young, and he'd collected enough timber over the years to build our own small teak house. Although life was simple, with no heating or electricity, I have fond memories of those early years.

We grew food on our own land surrounding the house. While rice was the major crop, we were lucky to have lots of different vegetables and herbs growing wild by the side of the rice paddy, so we often foraged for food. This bounty meant we rarely had to buy food from town, except for sugar and salt, which we used to ferment and preserve foods grown in the rainy season to use during the dry season.

I clearly remember the day an Australian visitor came to our house at the start of one rainy season, when the paddy was filled with water. As we walked home I noticed bubbles on the water, so I quickly put my hand underneath and caught some small freshwater crabs. My mother was very happy as we didn't have any meat or fish, and she used them to make her delicious tom yum crab. The visitor was really impressed with what we could cook from ingredients collected from the field and garden. I have happy memories of the times Mum and I went out into the bush at the end of the rainy season to search for local white shiitake-style mushrooms – they were hard to find, but we knew they grew in the same place every year. Considered a delicacy, they were expensive, so we sold them to increase our income.

There wasn't much food during the dry season, so Dad worked in the forest and Mum often went with a group of women from the village to search for freshwater fish in the nearby waterways. My grandfather provided bamboo coops and containers for them. We'd wait for Mum to return – if she was late, our dinner was late, but if we were lucky, we had dinner early. Mum made the best *tom yum* mud-fish I've ever eaten, and my grandfather supplied the dry-roasted chilli the adults added.

Every day I walked three kilometres and back to a primary school in a neighbouring village. Soon after I started high school, my dad set up a chicken farm and, being the eldest, it was my job to get up really early, wake my brother and sister, and give water to the chickens, then feed them before heading off to school. My siblings weren't happy about this, but it meant we were well-fed. Another bonus was that the manure fertilised our farm, so we always had plenty of home-grown vegetables. We worked hard and were always busy, but this was a prosperous and happy time for my family.

As the oldest, it was also my responsibility to help out at home, so I learnt to cook when I was eight. My mother and grandparents taught me to use whatever ingredients were available to make a tasty meal. My first lesson was how to cook rice over charcoal heat – later, we used an aluminium steamer and cake tin over charcoal or a gas burner. Mastering a simple stir-fry was next; even now, this is the style of dish my family enjoys most, especially my basil minced chicken on page 79.

When the work in the rice fields was done, we needed other sources of income. Mum and I cooked and sold food at the local night market, particularly during festivals and ceremonies at the temples. We sometimes worked from 6 p.m. to 6 a.m. and were well known for having the best desserts and popular sweet snacks, such as banana fritters.

After completing the equivalent of my higher school certificate in mathematics and science, I studied accounting at a university in Bangkok, which I must confess I didn't like. Without telling my parents, I moved to an open university and studied science with a major in chemistry – I really wanted to study food and cooking, but there were no courses in Thailand at that time.

Later, I spent six years in the south of Thailand, where I really enjoyed learning about the local cuisine from my partner's mother and sister – I'll never forget how much they taught me. Southern food includes dishes with Buddhist and Islamic influences and is very different from the food I grew up with. Turmeric is a common ingredient, though it's not used much at all in the rest of Thailand, and I found this, along with the frequent use of super-fresh seafood and freshwater greens, really interesting. Southerners also use more coconut cream and coconut milk, and they favour the spices used in the neighbouring countries of Malaysia and Indonesia.

DISCOVERING AUSTRALIA

During this time an Australian teacher came to a nearby village and offered free English lessons. I really enjoyed this; he was the first foreigner I'd met and he introduced me to Australia. So when I decided to see more of the world in 1985, I started with Sydney and I loved it so much that I wanted to stay. I was able to fulfil my dream of studying hospitality while working fulltime at various hotels, and eventually became a Qantas international flight attendant.

In about 1990, my parents came to visit me. I remember Mum looking for the ingredients to make her special desserts, but back then the only place to find them all was Cabramatta and the area near Central Station in Sydney's CBD now known as 'Thaina Town'. After cooking over charcoal fires with no oven all her life, you can just imagine how luxurious she found cooking in my kitchen!

OPENING SPICE I AM

Opening a food business was my partner Padet Nagsalab's idea. He liked my cooking and had the necessary financial skills to set up a business as he'd been a financial controller for an airway catering department. In April 2004 we opened the first Spice I Am restaurant in Surry Hills, with eight tables and eighteen chairs. We decided not to tone down, modify or substitute ingredients to suit local tastes, but to offer authentic Thai food cooked in the traditional way. We produced our own curry pastes and used the correct hot chillies to maintain the true flavour. This commitment to authenticity proved incredibly popular – the restaurant received rave reviews and is still operating as successfully as ever today.

In 2008, we opened a second Spice I Am in Darlinghurst. The idea was for more sophisticated, leisurely dining in an elegant space with an upscale cocktail bar and private room – in contrast to Surry Hills, which was a quick in-and-out BYO diner. In 2010 we opened House Thai in Surry Hills, specialising in Issan-style dishes, which are very lean as they don't include coconut milk, and feature the distinct flavour of fermented fish sauce. The food was hot, the atmosphere was laidback and the media loved it. We then opened Spice I Am Balmain, which has a fresh, young vibe and smart bar with the same delicious authentic Thai cuisine. Our most recent restaurant is Surry Hills Eating House, which draws on influences from southern Thai cooking.

Fortunately, most of the Thai vegetables and herbs we use in the restaurants are now available locally in the warmer months, and from Darwin or far-north Queensland during winter. The herbs must be fresh to provide the full flavour, aroma and pungency in the nose as you eat them. I also have a little farm in the Southern Highlands of NSW that now supplies kaffir limes and leaves for the restaurants and most of our greens.

SHARING TREASURED FAMILY RECIPES

Now, I am lucky to fulfil another dream – writing my own cookbook. Here, I share the recipes that I learnt at my mother's and grandparents' side, as well as those I discovered when living with my in-laws in Phuket. I'm also inspired by the different ingredients and techniques from the regions across Thailand, where the local climate and seasonal availability of ingredients strongly influence the food. In the north, for example, little or no coconut milk or cream is used, while animal fat and pork meat feature extensively due to the Chinese influence. Fresh herbs and spices are another common feature, thanks to the proximity to Laos and Vietnam. In the north-east, the cuisine is leaner, and dill and lemon basil star in many dishes. In central Thailand, one can find dishes from all areas of Thailand, so there is a much wider selection.

In Thailand, food is created to be communal. A selection of dishes is placed on the table at the same time and everyone happily shares them. Usually, there will be a stir-fry, curry, soup and fresh or steamed vegetables offered with a chilli dipping sauce. While steamed long-grain rice is served in most of Thailand, sticky rice is common in the north and north-east. These days, forks and spoons are used, but when I was young we used our fingers. At our restaurants we prefer to serve all our dishes to be shared, as is the tradition, and the chapters in the book reflect this respect for authenticity.

Traditionally, our meals don't start with an entree, but sometimes light snacks or small dishes are served in between the larger dishes. These smaller dishes used to take quite a long time to prepare, but now they've been adapted to be easier, and I've included some of these in the Light Meals chapter on pages 6–23. Mum always made a huge batch of these because of the large size of our family, and as kids we always looked forward to them. They looked and tasted so intriguing, and made me want to learn more about food.

In Thailand, soups (see pages 24–41) are not usually served separately, but dished up as a part of the main meal to be shared with rice. They are called *tom*, which means boiling water with added herbs, spices and protein. The same key ingredients are used throughout Thailand, but the proportion and preparation varies. Northern Thai cooks tend to use less chilli and more oily ingredients, and include fermented soybean paste instead of shrimp paste. In the north-east, coconut milk isn't used at all and sometimes raw ingredients are roasted before adding to the soup. In the south, cooks may include fresh turmeric in their broth. All these techniques are used in central Thailand, but the soups often include freshwater fish or scampi. Here in Australia, the most well-known Thai soup would have to be the hot and sour soup, *tom yum goong*, on page 31.

The rice and noodle dishes on pages 42–63 are made with ingredients you'll find at most greengrocers and supermarkets across Australia. The plain flavour of rice and noodles are enhanced by combining them with chilli for heat, tamarind or lime for sourness palm sugar for sweetness and oyster and soy sauces for salt. Quick and easy, they're ideal for a meal-on-the-run or a tasty snack. Most recipes can be made vegetarian by omitting the meat and oyster sauce. You can leave out the fish sauce too, but you'll need to add more salt. I suggest you taste as you cook and adjust the flavour as you go. Although a wok makes cooking Thai food simpler, it isn't essential – Mum made extremely good pad Thai (see page 55) when she first visited Sydney using a cast-iron frying pan.

Our table always includes a salad – they're easy and refreshing, and the flavours dance in your mouth. The idea is to achieve a balance of salty, sweet and sour with heat from chilli. Be careful not to add too much fish sauce, as it easily overpowers other ingredients; sometimes you may need to season with salt to maintain the right balance and not make the dressing too liquid. Similarly, cane sugar can be added with the palm sugar to get the correct balance of sweetness. I find the softer palm sugar produces the best balance, but the harder palm sugar, which usually has added cane sugar and is therefore sweeter, can be used instead. Tahitian lime is included for sourness – lemon can be substituted, but it doesn't produce a well-balanced result.

Each meal also includes a stir-fry (see pages 64–89) of one kind or another. Mum told me that cooking oil wasn't available when she was young, so they simply tossed vegetables in the wok till they were cooked. Stir-fries were my grandfather's specialty. In his generation, meat came from wild animals and cooking oil wasn't used at all; the fat generated from the meat as it cooked was used instead. Homemade fish sauce was the only seasoning, and no sugar was added – the balance of flavours came from the ingredients, which always included organic homegrown vegetables. Although we now cook with a wide range of meats, these principles are still maintained in the kitchen at Spice I Am.

Having conquered stir-fries, Mum taught me how to cook a coconut-based curry. The first step was grinding fresh coconut flesh to make coconut cream. Next was making the curry pastes from scratch (see pages 180–186). She taught me to prepare all the ingredients before starting to cook, as the process is so quick. Once the charcoal fire was lit, it was so hot it was used to steam the rice, then the rest of the meal was cooked with the remaining heat.

There are two types of Thai curry: coconut-based curries are made by cooking curry paste with fresh coconut cream or vegetable oil until you have a rich aroma, so all the paste ingredients are well cooked before adding the meat. The meat is then cooked until it has absorbed the flavour of the paste. This is the traditional way to make a Thai curry, passed down over generations, and it's the way that I pass on here. Water-based curries use water or stock instead of coconut, and are therefore much lighter, but also spicier, with a sweet-and-sour note.

When seasoning a curry, add the fish sauce, then taste to see if you need to add any sugar. Vegetables add a wonderful texture to the dish. Sweet basil gives a lovely perfume that's especially important in coconut-based curries, whereas water-based curries tend to include hot basil or holy basil. Wild basil works well with wild or strong meats such as lamb or boar.

On pages 138–155 I've included some of my favourite special Thai dishes. Traditionally, these weren't everyday meals, but prepared during important cultural events and religious ceremonies. Some are only made when the ingredients are seasonally available, and different parts of the country have their own specialties depending on the tribe, culture and local ingredients. Most children look forward to these occasions and the food that went with them – I know I did! Nowadays, these dishes are so popular you don't have to wait for a special occasion to enjoy them.

Dessert as we know it in Australia is not often served in Thailand – usually a selection of fresh fruit is offered at the end of a meal instead. Mum sometimes served sweets as a treat when all of us kids were home, however Dad got used to having dessert, so we now enjoy it regularly (thanks, Dad!). My mother's recipes for my childhood favourites can be found on pages 156–171.

I love to cook more than anything else, and cooking the food I grew up with is my passion. I learnt early on how to cook a meal to nourish and give pleasure to my family from whatever we found in the paddy fields, and I carry these valuable lessons with me to this day. My hope is that sharing my treasured family recipes here will inspire you to cook Thai food at home, too.

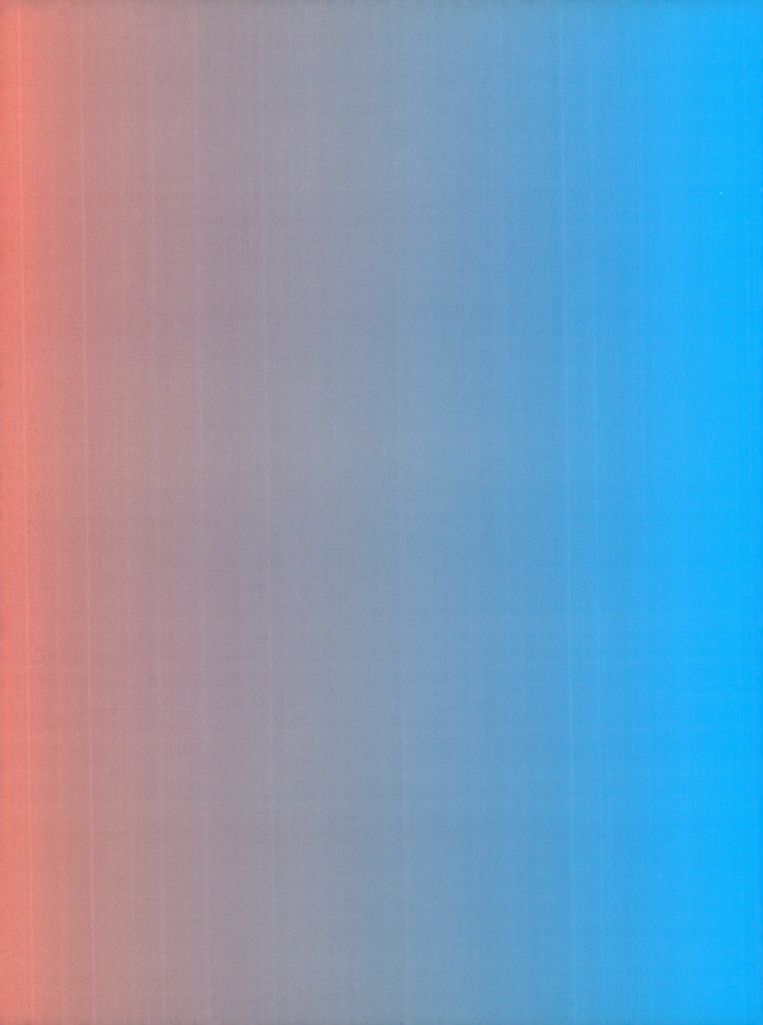

LIGHT MEALS

HUA PLEE TOD
BANANA FLOWER CAKES

MAKES 4

When I was young, this was a popular homemade vegetarian dish, as banana flowers were cheap and readily available, and it is quick to both prepare and cook.

1 banana flower, trimmed
50 g rice flour
1½ tablespoons Red Curry Paste (see page 184)
1 egg, lightly beaten
50 ml coconut milk
50 ml water

1½ tablespoons fish sauce
2 kaffir lime leaves, julienned
3 sprigs holy basil (see page 194)
2 teaspoons white sugar
vegetable oil, for deep-frying
50 g coarsely crushed unsalted cashews
Sweet Chilli Sauce (see page 187), to serve

Remove the outer purple leaves and any unformed bananas from the banana flower until a firm white core is revealed. Wash the core thoroughly, then julienne.

Place the banana flower, rice flour, red curry paste, egg, coconut milk, water, fish sauce, kaffir lime leaf, 2 holy basil leaves and sugar in a bowl and mix with a large metal spoon. Divide into quarters, then shape into flat cakes.

Heat vegetable oil for deep-frying in a deep-fryer or deep heavy-based saucepan until it reaches 160°C on a sugar/deep-fry thermometer. Deep-fry the banana flower cakes for 1 minute on the first side, then turn and fry for another 1 minute on the other side. Turn again and cook for another 30 seconds or until cooked through and golden. Remove with a slotted spoon and drain on paper towel. Deep-fry the remaining holy basil sprigs for 20 seconds, then remove and drain on paper towel.

Transfer the cakes to a serving plate and scatter with the cashews and crisp basil leaves, then serve with the sweet chilli sauce.

TOD MUN PLA

DEEP-FRIED FISHCAKES WITH SWEET CHILLI SAUCE

MAKES 6

Fishcakes are one of the best known dishes in Thai cu sine, and are popular all over Thailand. Each part of Thailand has a different name for these delicious morsels, but they all include the same ingredients cooked using different techniques. They are wonderful eaten by themselves, or can be served with Thai sweet chilli sauce or peanut sauce for dipping, if you like.

300 g red fish fillets, minced
30 g Red Curry Paste (see page 184)
1 teaspoon sugar
1 tablespoon fish sauce
1 egg, lightly beaten
3 kaffir lime leaves, julienned
4–5 green beans, thinly sliced
2–3 sprigs holy basil (see page 194),
    roughly chopped

10 g fresh or rinsed and drained pickled
    krachai (see page 194), thinly sliced
200 ml vegetable oil, for deep-frying
Sweet Chilli Sauce (see page 187) tossed
    with sliced cucumber, coriander leaves,
    thinly sliced red shallots, sliced long
    red chilli and crushed roasted
    unsalted peanuts
Peanut Sauce (see page 188), to serve

Place the minced fish, curry paste, sugar, fish sauce and egg in a bowl and mix to combine well. Add the kaffir lime leaves, beans, bas l and krachai and stir to combine. Divide the fish mixture into 6 equal portions and, using wet hands, form each one into a ball, then flatten slightly and set aside.

Heat the vegetable oil in a deep-fryer or deep heavy-based saucepan until it reaches 160°C on a sugar/deep-fry thermometer, then deep-fry the fish cakes until golden and cooked through. Remove the fritters with a slotted spoon and drain on paper towel.

Serve the fish cakes garnished with sweet chilli sauce mixed with cucumber, coriander, red shallot, chilli and peanuts, and peanut sauce to the side.

PLA TOD PHAE
CURRIED FISH FRITTERS

MAKES ABOUT 16

This dish reminds me of home, as my grandfather was an expert at catching freshwater fish in the waterways around our village. Freshly caught freshwater whitebait mixed with red curry paste and a touch of rice flour, then seasoned with homemade fish sauce – you can't ask for more than that! In Australia, silver bait is easy to get, and fresh Australian whitebait is available in June and July.

250 g silver bait or whitebait
100 g Red Curry Paste (see page 184)
¼ cup (60 ml) fish sauce
⅔ cup (100 g) rice flour
⅓ cup (80 ml) Lime Water (see page 178)
1 egg, lightly beaten

4–5 sprigs holy basil (see page 194)
3 kaffir lime leaves, julienned
vegetable oil, for deep-frying
Sweet Chilli Sauce (see page 187),
   julienned long red chilli and
   coriander leaves, to serve

Place the fish in a bowl and add the curry paste, fish sauce, rice flour, lime water and egg and mix using clean, wet hands. Add the basil and kaffir lime and mix to combine well.

Heat vegetable oil for deep-drying in a deep-fryer or deep heavy-based saucepan until it reaches 160°C on a sugar/deep-fry thermometer. Working in batches, add heaped tablespoonfuls of the mixture to the pan and fry a few fritters at a time, turning, for 3–5 minutes or until golden brown. Remove the fritters with a slotted spoon and drain on paper towel.

Serve the fritters at room temperature, scattered with coriander leaves and drizzled with sweet chilli sauce.

TOD MUN GOONG
PRAWN CAKES

MAKES ABOUT 15

The prawns add texture to the fritters, so don't chop them too finely. These cook really quickly and taste best when served straight from the pan, so have your guests assembled and ready to eat before you start frying.

500 g raw prawn meat, coarsely minced
100 g pork belly, coarsely minced
3 cloves garlic, peeled
1 coriander root, well washed
1 tablespoon white peppercorns
2 teaspoons salt
1 tablespoon light soy sauce

2 teaspoons white sugar
1 tablespoon tapioca flour (see page 195)
1 tablespoon vegetable oil, plus extra
    for deep-frying
handful coriander leaves, finely chopped
Sweet Chilli Sauce (see page 187), to serve

Combine the prawn and pork mince in a bowl, cover with plastic film and refrigerate for 30 minutes to chill and firm.

Meanwhile, place the garlic, coriander root, peppercorns and salt in a mortar and use the pestle to crush to a fine paste. Set aside.

Add the garlic paste, light soy sauce, sugar, tapioca flour, 1 tablespoon vegetable oil and coriander to the prawn and pork mixture. Using a wet wooden spoon, blend the mixture for 5 minutes until well combined. Divide into 15 balls (about 50 g each), then flatten slightly.

Heat vegetable oil for deep-frying in a deep-fryer or deep heavy-based saucepan until it reaches 160°C on a sugar/deep-fry thermometer. Working in batches, deep-fry the prawn cakes for 5–6 minutes or until cooked through and golden. Remove the prawn cakes with a slotted spoon and drain on paper towel. Serve immediately with sweet chilli sauce.

MOO PING
CHARGRILLED PORK SKEWERS

SERVES 8 AS PART OF A SHARED MEAL

Ping is the Issan word for grilling, and these grilled pork skewers are a common breakfast dish for kids before they go to school. It is often found at street-food stalls throughout Thailand, and is best eaten with steamed sticky rice. If you like a bit of fat, then boneless pork belly can be used instead of fillets. This recipe needs to be started the day before you wish to serve it, as the pork tastes better after marinating in the fridge overnight.

600 g lean pork fillet, cut into
   12 cm × 2 cm strips
5–6 coriander roots, well washed
   and chopped
1 teaspoon freshly ground white pepper
8 large cloves garlic, peeled
140 g soft palm sugar

¼ cup (60 ml) light soy sauce
¼ cup (60 ml) oyster sauce
1 teaspoon dark soy sauce
Steamed Sticky Rice (see page 187),
   to serve
Tamarind *Jim Jaew* Dipping Sauce
   (see page 191), to serve

Place the pork in a bowl.

Place the coriander roots, pepper, garlic and palm sugar in a mortar and use the pestle to crush to a coarse paste. Stir in the light soy sauce, oyster sauce and dark soy sauce until well mixed. Pour the marinade over the pork and turn to coat the pork evenly. Cover with plastic film and refrigerate overnight.

Soak sixteen 15 cm bamboo skewers in water for 15–30 minutes, then remove and thread the pork onto the skewers.

Preheat a barbecue grill plate or chargrill pan to high heat. Cook the pork skewers on the hot barbecue or chargrill for 5–6 minutes on each side or until cooked, then serve with sticky rice and tamarind *jim jaew* dipping sauce.

SATAY GAI
MY CHICKEN SATAY

SERVES 8 AS PART OF A SHARED MEAL

In Thailand, it is common to find this cooked with pork instead of chicken, but in my opinion, chicken tenderloins provide the best experience of this popular dish.

100 ml coconut cream
100 ml evaporated milk
1 tablespoon vegetable oil
100 g soft palm sugar
2 teaspoons salt

¼ cup (30 g) medium curry powder
1 teaspoon ground turmeric
20 (about 1 kg) chicken breast tenderloins
Peanut Sauce (see page 188), to serve
Cucumber Relish (see page 192), to serve

Place the coconut cream, evaporated milk, vegetable oil, palm sugar, salt, curry powder and turmeric in a bowl and stir until well combined.

Place the chicken in a large bowl, then pour the marinade over and turn to coat. Cover with plastic film and marinate in the fridge for at least 30 minutes for the flavours to develop.

Meanwhile, soak twenty 16 cm bamboo skewers in water for 15–30 minutes, then drain. Thread the chicken onto the skewers.

Preheat a barbecue grill plate or chargrill pan to medium heat. Cook the chicken skewers on the hot barbecue or chargrill, turning, for 6–8 minutes or until they are cooked through.

Serve the chicken satay with peanut sauce and cucumber relish alongside.

NUA DAED DEAW
'SUN-DRIED' BEEF

SERVES 4 AS PART OF A SHARED MEAL

Hailing from the north-east of Thailand, this popular dish is renowned for its rich, spicy flavour, making it a perfect accompaniment for steamed sticky rice. Traditionally, the marinated beef was left to dry in the sun for a day, then cooked on the following day, but I have modified the cooking method for Australian kitchens. It is best served at room temperature, so it is a great recipe to prepare in advance, then bring out when your guests arrive.

1 × 500 g piece topside beef, cut into
   6 cm-long × 1 cm-wide slices
1 teaspoon crushed black peppercorns
1 teaspoon crushed coriander seeds
2 teaspoons white sugar
1½ tablespoons Thai seasoning sauce
   (see page 195)
3 teaspoons fish sauce

1½ tablespoons vegetable oil, plus
   extra for deep-frying
5 kaffir lime leaves, lightly fried
Steamed Sticky Rice (see page 187),
   to serve
Tamarind *Jim Jaew* Dipping Sauce
   (see page 191), to serve

Place the beef in a mixing bowl, then add the pepper, coriander seeds, sugar, seasoning sauce, fish sauce and 1½ tablespoons vegetable oil. Mix well, then cover with plastic film and leave to marinate in the fridge for at least 30 minutes, or overnight, if you have time.

Heat vegetable oil for deep-frying in a deep-fryer or deep heavy-based saucepan until it reaches 160°C on a sugar/deep-fry thermometer. Working in batches, deep-fry the beef for 4 minutes, turning continuously. Remove from the pan using tongs and drain on paper towel. Garnish with fried kaffir lime leaves and serve with steamed sticky rice and tamarind dipping sauce to the side.

SOUPS

HOY MAENG PHOO OB
STEAMED BLACK MUSSEL SOUP

SERVES 4 AS PART OF A SHARED MEAL

This simple, fresh soup is popular throughout Thailand, served for either lunch or dinner. Thai mussels are small, green, and very similar to New Zealand green mussels – although only half the size. The heat of the chilli and the fragrant Thai sweet basil make this mussel soup to-die-for. Note that it's not a very brothy soup.

1 kg black mussels, cleaned and bearded
1 large stick lemongrass, cut into
   8 cm lengths
5 kaffir lime leaves, torn
10 red birds-eye chillies, bruised

150 ml hot water
1 tablespoon fish sauce
5–6 sprigs Thai sweet basil
Seafood Dipping Sauce (see page 191),
   to serve

Add a couple of tablespoons of water to just cover the base of a large heavy-based saucepan and bring to the boil over high heat. Add the mussels and quickly shake the pan. Add the lemongrass, kaffir lime leaves, chillies, hot water and fish sauce. Cover the pan and cook the mussels for 3–4 minutes, shaking the pan occasionally. Remove the lid, add three-quarters of the sweet basil leaves and stir; the mussels are ready when they have opened.

Serve the mussel mixture garnished with the remaining basil leaves and with the seafood dipping sauce alongside.

TOM YUM GOONG
HOT & SPICY SOUP WITH PRAWNS

SERVES 6 AS PART OF A SHARED MEAL

This is probably the best-known Thai soup around the world. In Thailand, it is traditional to use freshwater scampi or marron, but larger raw king prawns are suitable too. Each cook uses their own finishing touch to achieve the all-important balance of hot, sour and salty – mine is to use a little evaporated milk.

12 large raw prawns, peeled and cleaned, heads and shells reserved
1 litre water
2 red shallots, peeled and bruised
1 large stick lemongrass, cut into 5 cm lengths
1 × 60 g piece galangal (see page 194), sliced
100 g oyster mushrooms, torn

100 ml fish sauce
2 tablespoons Chilli Jam (see page 188)
¼ cup (60 ml) lime juice
50 ml evaporated milk
5 kaffir lime leaves, torn
6 red birds-eye chillies, bruised
10 sprigs coriander, roughly chopped
8–10 sprigs Vietnamese coriander (see page 195), roughly chopped

Place the prawn heads in a mortar and use the pestle to crush. Bring the water to the boil in a heavy-based saucepan and add the prawn heads and shells, then stir well. Bring back to the boil, then remove from the heat and strain the prawn stock through a fine-mesh sieve over a clean heavy-based saucepan, discarding the solids.

Bring the prawn stock to the boil again over medium heat. Add the shallots, lemongrass and galangal and return to the boil. Add the prawn flesh, mushrooms, fish sauce and chilli jam, then stir for 1–2 minutes or until the prawns are just cooked.

Remove the pan from the heat and add the lime juice, evaporated milk, kaffir lime leaves, chillies and most of the coriander and Vietnamese coriander. Stir well. Serve the soup garnished with the remaining coriander and Vietnamese coriander.

TOM YUM THI PLA HUA PHREE
HOT & SPICY FISH SOUP

SERVES 4–5 AS PART OF A SHARED MEAL

When I was a child, my mother often cooked this during the dry season, after first catching the fish in the shallow creek near our home. One fish was enough to feed us all, and banana flower was added for extra texture and body. The whole family enjoyed this satisfying spicy soup.

5 large cloves garlic, peeled
15 small dried red chillies
2 large red shallots, tops and bases trimmed
600 ml coconut milk
1 banana flower (about 160–180 g), trimmed
1 × 50 g piece galangal (see page 194), sliced
1 large stick lemongrass, cut into 5 cm lengths
⅓ cup (80 ml) fish sauce

2 tablespoons tamarind puree (see page 195)
2 tablespoons white sugar
500 g bar cod, blue-eye trevalla or other firm white fish fillets, skin removed and cut into bite-sized pieces
100 g oyster mushrooms, torn
1 tablespoon lime juice
5 kaffir lime leaves, torn
10 sprigs coriander, roughly chopped
5 red birds-eye chillies, bruised

Toss the garlic cloves in a dry small frying pan over medium heat until soft on the outside. Remove and set aside. Toss the dried chillies in the pan over medium heat until slightly scorched and aromatic. Dry-roast the shallots in the pan until slightly softened, then peel and gently bruise. Set aside.

Place the garlic, shallots and 5 of the fried chillies in a mortar and use the pestle to pound to a coarse paste.

Remove the outer purple leaves and any unformed bananas from the banana flower until a firm white core is revealed. Wash the core thoroughly, then cut into 5 cm lengths. Place the coconut milk and banana flower in a heavy-based saucepan and bring to the boil over medium heat. Add the chilli paste, galangal and lemongrass and cook for 5 minutes, stirring often. Add the fish sauce, tamarind puree, sugar, fish and oyster mushrooms and cook for 4–5 minutes or until the fish is just cooked through.

Remove the pan from the heat and stir in the lime juice, kaffir lime leaves and half of the coriander. Crush another 5 of the fried chillies with the mortar and pestle and add to the soup with the birds-eye chillies, then stir well.

Garnish the soup with the remaining coriander and fried chillies and serve.

TOM KHA GAI
CHICKEN, COCONUT & GALANGAL SOUP

SERVES 4 AS PART OF A SHARED MEAL

Tom kha gai is the coconut-based soup common in the central part of Thailand. Simply made with coconut milk, herbs, chilli and fish sauce, some areas do not add lime juice but use tamarind puree instead to add that vital hint of sourness. Chilli powder can be added to increase the heat, if you like more spice.

8 small dried red chillies
600 ml coconut milk
200 ml chicken stock
1 teaspoon white sugar
1 large stick lemongrass, cut into 8 cm lengths
1 × 60 g piece galangal (see page 194), peeled and thinly sliced
2 large red shallots, peeled and bruised
300 g chicken breast fillet, thinly sliced on the diagonal

100 g oyster mushrooms, torn
¼ cup (60 ml) fish sauce
2 tablespoons tamarind puree (see page 195)
6 red birds-eye chillies, bruised
1 tablespoon lime juice
5 kaffir lime leaves, torn
12 sprigs coriander, roughly chopped
10 sprigs Vietnamese coriander (see page 195), cut into 1–2 cm lengths

Toss the dried chillies in a dry heavy-based frying pan over medium heat until slightly scorched and aromatic. Place 4 of the chillies in a mortar and crush with the pestle.

Combine the coconut milk, chicken stock and sugar in a large heavy-based saucepan and stir over medium heat. When the mixture comes to the boil, add the lemongrass, galangal and shallots and stir to combine. Add the chicken, mushrooms, fish sauce, tamarind puree and birds-eye chillies and reduce the heat to low, then simmer for about 4 minutes or until the chicken is cooked through.

Remove the pan from the heat and add the lime juice, 4 of the kaffir lime leaves, 8 coriander sprigs and 6 sprigs of the Vietnamese coriander. Add the crushed chilli to the soup, then stir well.

Garnish the soup with the remaining coriander, Vietnamese coriander, kaffir lime leaf and fried chillies, and serve.

TOM YUM GAI
HOT & SPICY CHICKEN SOUP

SERVES 4 AS PART OF A SHARED MEAL

This is another dish renowned throughout Thailand. While different regions use slightly different ingredients, the resulting flavour is almost the same – hot and sour is the key. I use a whole spatchcock when I make this recipe as it adds a welcome touch of sweetness to the soup.

12 large cloves garlic, peeled
15 small dried chillies
2 red shallots, tops and bases trimmed
1 × 500 g spatchcock, jointed into 8 pieces
1 litre water
100 g oyster mushrooms, torn
1 large stick lemongrass, cut into
  8 cm lengths
1 × 60 g piece galangal (see page 194), sliced

⅓ cup (80 ml) fish sauce
¼ cup (60 ml) tamarind puree
  (see page 195)
8–10 sprigs Vietnamese coriander
  (see page 195), roughly chopped
8 kaffir lime leaves, torn
6 sprigs holy basil (see page 194)

Toss the garlic cloves in a dry small frying pan over medium heat until soft on the outside. Remove and set aside. Toss the dried chillies in the frying pan over medium heat until slightly scorched and aromatic. Dry-roast the shallots in the pan over medium heat until slightly softened, then peel and gently bruise. Set aside.

Place the spatchcock in a heavy-based saucepan and add the water. Bring to the boil over medium heat, then add the oyster mushrooms, lemongrass, galangal, shallots, garlic and dried chillies. Reduce the heat to medium and simmer for 5–6 minutes or until the spatchcock pieces are cooked through.

Add the fish sauce and tamarind puree and stir well. Remove from the heat and stir in the Vietnamese coriander, kaffir lime leaves and 3 of the holy basil sprigs.

Serve the soup garnished with the remaining holy basil sprigs.

TOM MA RA KA DOOK MOO
BITTER MELON SOUP WITH PORK RIBS

SERVES 6–8 AS PART OF A SHARED MEAL

My family loves this soup so much that it is one of the special dishes we must have when we get together back home in Thailand. My mother says that fresh whole white peppercorns are the key to this comforting dish. As you eat the soup, the kick of pepper hits your palate and clears the airways. It is best to use larger bitter melons for this, if you can, as they have a better flavour than the smaller ones.

12 large cloves garlic, peeled

5–6 coriander roots, well washed

1 teaspoon white peppercorns

500 g pork spare ribs, cut into 3-bone sections

600 g large bitter melons, halved lengthways, seeds and inner white flesh removed and discarded, cut into 6 cm-long pieces

8 dried shiitake mushrooms

2.5 litres water

⅔ cup (160 ml) light soy sauce

2 tablespoons Thai seasoning sauce (see page 195)

2 tablespoons oyster sauce

Place 6 cloves of garlic, the coriander roots and peppercorns in a mortar and use the pestle to crush to a coarse paste.

Place the pork, bitter melon, mushrooms, remaining cloves of garlic and garlic mixture in a large heavy-based saucepan or stockpot. Add the water, soy sauce, seasoning sauce and oyster sauce and stir well. Bring to the boil over high heat, then reduce the heat to low. Cover and simmer over low heat for 35 minutes without removing the lid; the pork and bitter melon should be tender.

Serve immediately.

TOM NUA TOUN
SPICY SLOW-COOKED BEEF SOUP

SERVES 4 AS PART OF A SHARED MEAL

This aromatic, rich soup reminds me of my grandfather, who was regarded as the best at cooking beef in our family. He always used very fresh beef and preferred to cook it really slowly. The beef we get in Australia is very suitable for making this family favourite.

2 large red shallots, tops and bases trimmed
400 g Slow-cooked Beef (see page 176)
2 cups (500 ml) water
¼ cup (60 ml) fish sauce
2 tablespoons tamarind puree (see page 195)
1 large stick lemongrass, cut into 8 cm lengths and leaf section tied into a knot

1 × 50 g piece galangal (see page 194), sliced
10 red birds-eye chillies, bruised
8–10 sprigs Vietnamese coriander (see page 195), cut into 1.5-cm lengths
5 kaffir lime leaves, torn
4 sprigs Thai sweet basil (see page 195)
1 tablespoon lime juice

Dry-roast the shallots in a dry small frying pan over medium heat until softened. Peel and gently bruise, then set aside.

Place the slow-cooked beef and water in a heavy-based saucepan and bring to the boil over medium heat. Reduce the heat to low and simmer for 3–4 minutes. Add the fish sauce and tamarind puree and stir well. Add the lemongrass, galangal and shallots and cook for 5–6 minutes, then add the birds-eye chillies and stir well.

Remove the pan from the heat and add three-quarters of the Vietnamese coriander, the kaffir lime leaves and 3 sprigs of the basil. Stir well and add the lime juice.

Stir again and serve garnished with the remaining Vietnamese coriander and basil.

RICE AND NOODLES

KHAO PAD GAI
THAI FRIED RICE WITH CHICKEN

SERVES 3–4 AS PART OF A SHARED MEAL

Fried rice is a great way of turning leftover cooked rice into another hearty meal. Nowadays it is served as a meal in its own right, but when I was young it was made for the family to share so as not to waste any food, and usually served up on the table alongside a selection of other dishes. Each cook has a different recipe, depending on what they have in their fridge or pantry. For me, sweet brown onions and tomatoes are important, and I like to offer sliced cucumber and a lime wedge to the side.

2 tablespoons vegetable oil
2 large cloves garlic, finely chopped
120 g chicken breast fillet, thinly sliced
   on the diagonal
½ small onion, thinly sliced
2 eggs, lightly beaten
1 tablespoon light soy sauce
1 tablespoon Thai seasoning
   sauce (see page 195)

200 g cold cooked jasmine rice
6 cherry tomatoes, halved
2 spring onions, cut into 5 cm lengths
freshly ground white pepper
¼ lebanese cucumber, sliced
coriander sprigs and lime wedges,
   to serve

Heat the vegetable oil in a wok or large heavy-based frying pan over medium heat. Add the garlic and stir for 1 minute, then add the chicken and stir-fry for 4 minutes or until it is cooked through. Remove the chicken and set aside. Add the onion to the wok and stir well. Add the egg and stir for 1 minute or until cooked, then add the soy sauce and seasoning sauce and stir to combine.

Add the cold rice, cherry tomatoes, spring onion and chicken and stir for 2–3 minutes or until the rice and chicken are evenly heated through. Season with white pepper and remove from the heat.

Serve the rice garnished with cucumber, coriander and lime wedges.

KHAO PAD KEE MAO GAI
SPICY FRIED RICE WITH CHICKEN

SERVES 4 AS PART OF A SHARED MEAL

This tasty version of fried rice is spicy from the fresh chilli, which, along with the holy basil, really enhances its flavour. The heat level can be adjusted by adding more or less chilli.

190 ml vegetable oil
4–5 sprigs holy basil (see page 194)
2 large cloves garlic, finely chopped
3 red birds-eye chillies, finely chopped
120 g chicken breast fillet, thinly sliced on the diagonal
2 eggs, lightly beaten

1 tablespoon light soy sauce
1 tablespoon Thai seasoning sauce (see page 195)
1 teaspoon white sugar
400 g cold cooked jasmine rice
3 large fresh red chillies, thinly sliced on the diagonal

Pour 150 ml of the vegetable oil into a small heavy-based saucepan and heat over medium heat. When the oil is hot, add 2 sprigs of the holy basil leaves and deep-fry for 10–20 seconds until crisp. Remove with a slotted spoon and drain on paper towel.

Heat the remaining vegetable oil in a large wok or large heavy-based frying pan over medium heat. Add the garlic and birds-eye chilli and stir for 1–2 minutes, then add the chicken and stir-fry for 4 minutes or until the chicken is cooked through. Remove the chicken and set aside.

Add the egg to the wok and stir for 1 minute or until cooked. Add the soy sauce, seasoning sauce and sugar and stir to combine. Add the cold rice, cooked chicken and two-thirds of the sliced chilli and stir for 2–3 minutes or until the rice and chicken are heated through. Add the remaining holy basil leaves, then stir and remove from the heat. Garnish with the fried basil leaves and the remaining sliced chilli, then serve.

KHAO PAD PHU
FRIED RICE WITH CRAB

SERVES 6 AS PART OF A SHARED MEAL

Adding fresh crab meat to fried rice gives it a delicate flavour and aroma – be careful not to add too much white pepper as it can overpower the sweetness of the crab.

⅓ cup (80 ml) vegetable oil
4 large cloves garlic, chopped
2 eggs, lightly beaten
1 tablespoon light soy sauce
1 tablespoon Thai seasoning
  sauce (see page 195)
1 teaspoon white sugar
500 g cold cooked jasmine rice

200 g cooked crab meat (available from
  good-quality fishmongers), picked over
  to remove any shell
½ teaspoon freshly ground white pepper
3 spring onions, thinly sliced
½ small lebanese cucumber, sliced
coriander leaves and lime wedges,
  to serve

Heat the vegetable oil in a wok or large heavy-based frying pan over medium heat. Add the garlic and stir for 1 minute, then reduce the heat to low. Add the egg and stir for 1 minute or until cooked. Add the soy sauce, seasoning sauce, sugar and cold rice and stir well. Add the crab and stir for 2–3 minutes until the rice and crab are heated through. Season with the white pepper and add the spring onion, then stir to combine.

Serve the rice garnished with cucumber, coriander and lime wedges.

PAD MEE

STIR-FRIED VERMICELLI WITH BEAN CURD

SERVES 6 AS PART OF A SHARED MEAL

This noodle dish is traditionally served at large functions. The person who cooks it must be skilful, as they need to know when the noodles are cooked properly and not too soft. The use of Thai dried rice vermicelli noodles is the key to success.

4 large dried chillies
1 large red shallot, sliced
150 g dried rice vermicelli
2 cups (500 ml) water
2 eggs, lightly beaten
¼ cup (60 ml) vegetable oil
1½ tablespoons fish sauce
2 tablespoons soft palm sugar
2 tablespoons tamarind puree
  (see page 195)

80 g firm bean curd (tofu), diced
2½ spring onions, cut into 5 cm lengths
1–2 teaspoons chilli powder, to taste
1 teaspoon white sugar
⅓ cup (45 g) roasted unsalted peanuts,
  finely ground
100 g bean sprouts
6 sprigs coriander, cut into 5 cm lengths
1 large fresh red chilli, julienned (optional)

Soak the dried chillies in a small bowl of warm water for 3–4 minutes, then drain. Place the soaked chillies and shallot in a mortar and use the pestle to pound to a coarse paste. Place the vermicelli in a bowl and cover with cold water, then leave for 10 minutes to soften. Drain and set aside.

Place the water in a heavy-based saucepan and bring to the boil over medium heat. Add the drained vermicelli and stir briefly until the water returns to the boil, then drain the vermicelli and set aside.

Heat a dry non-stick frying pan over medium heat, then add the egg and cook until it is just cooked; it should be an omelette. Transfer to a plate and leave to cool slightly, then cut into 5 mm-thick strips.

Heat the vegetable oil in a wok or large heavy-based frying pan over medium heat. Add the chilli and shallot paste and stir for 1–2 minutes. Add the fish sauce, palm sugar and tamarind puree and cook for 1–2 minutes. Add the drained vermicelli and cook, stirring, for 2–3 minutes, then add the bean curd, spring onion and cooked egg and stir well. Sprinkle in the chilli powder and sugar and stir to combine. Add half of the ground peanuts and remove the wok from the heat.

Add half each of the bean sprouts and coriander and toss gently. Garnish the vermicelli with the remaining bean sprouts, coriander and ground peanuts. Top with the julienned chilli, if you like, and serve.

PAD THAI

SERVES 6 AS PART OF A SHARED MEAL

Probably the most well-known Thai noodle dish, *pad Thai* is really easy to make at home even though it has lots of ingredients. The balance of sweet, salty and sour is very important, and I suggest that you use the amount of chilli you prefer. Some people worry about the quantity of dried shrimp, but don't leave it out, because not only is it key to the flavour of this dish, it also provides protein.

150 g dried thin rice stick noodles
¼ cup (60 ml) vegetable oil
6 raw king prawns, shelled and deveined
1 small red shallot, sliced
80 g firm bean curd (tofu) diced
50 g dried shrimp (see page 194)
¼ cup (60 ml) fish sauce
2 tablespoons soft palm sugar
2 tablespoons tamarind puree
  (see page 195)
1 teaspoon white vinegar

2–3 teaspoons chilli powder, to taste
2 eggs, lightly beaten
45 g roasted unsalted peanuts, finely
  ground
150 g bean sprouts
small handful garlic chives, cut into
  2 cm lengths
1 teaspoon white sugar
lime wedges and trimmed spring
  onion, to serve

Place the rice noodles in a bowl, cover with cold water and set aside for 1 hour, then drain.

Heat 2 tablespoons of the vegetable oil in a wok or large heavy-based frying pan over medium heat. Add the prawns and stir-fry for 2–3 minutes or until they just change colour, then remove and set aside. Add the shallot and stir-fry for 2–3 minutes or until tender, then add the bean curd and dried shrimp. Add the fish sauce, palm sugar and tamarind puree and cook for 1–2 minutes or until the sugar has dissolved.

Add the drained rice noodles and stir quickly so they don't stick to the bottom of the wok or pan. Add the vinegar and stir briefly. Add 1 teaspoon of the chilli powder and stir for 2–3 minutes. Reduce the heat to low, then carefully move the noodle mixture to one side of the wok or pan and add the remaining oil and egg, stirring to spread the egg over the base of the wok or pan. Fold the noodle mixture on top of the egg and stir well, scraping the egg off the base of the wok or pan until scrambled and cooked through.

Add half of the ground peanuts and stir, then remove from the heat. Add most of the bean sprouts and garlic chives and toss gently.

Top the noodles with the prawns and transfer to a serving plate or platter. Mix together the white sugar and remaining chilli powder. Place the remaining bean sprouts, chives, ground peanuts, sugar and chilli mixture, lime wedges and spring onion to the side of the noodles, then serve.

SEN YAI PAD KHEE MAO
SPICY NOODLES WITH PRAWNS

SERVES 4 AS PART OF A SHARED MEAL

Similar in flavouring to my spicy fried rice on page 48, this is made with noodles instead, as some people prefer the texture. Your guests will fall in love with this colourful and tasty dish. If you can't find holy basil, use Thai sweet basil instead.

¼ cup (60 ml) vegetable oil

4 large cloves garlic, chopped

3 birds-eye chillies, finely chopped

8 large raw king prawns, peeled and deveined, with tails intact

350 g fresh thick flat rice noodles

1 tablespoon fish sauce

1 tablespoon Thai seasoning sauce (see page 195)

1 tablespoon white sugar

1 teaspoon dark soy sauce

2 eggs, lightly beaten

3 large fresh red chillies, thinly sliced on the diagonal

100 g (about 2 large stems) Chinese broccoli (also known as gai lan), trimmed and cut into 4–5 cm lengths

4–5 sprigs holy basil (see page 194)

Heat the vegetable oil in a wok or large heavy-based frying pan over medium heat. Add the garlic and chilli and stir-fry for 1–2 minutes until fragrant. Add the prawns and cook for 1–2 minutes or until the prawns change colour. Add the noodles and stir to combine.

Add the fish sauce, seasoning sauce, sugar and dark soy sauce and cook for 1–2 minutes. Carefully move the noodle mixture to one side of the wok or pan, add the beaten egg to the other side and stir well, then fold the noodles on top of the egg. When the egg is cooked, add the sliced chilli, Chinese broccoli and holy basil and stir-fry for 1–2 minutes or until the broccoli is just tender.

Place the stir-fried noodles on a platter or individual serving plates and serve.

KUAY TEAW KHUA GAI

STIR-FRIED RICE NOODLES WITH CHICKEN

SERVES 4 AS PART OF A SHARED MEAL

This dish is similar in seasonings to the classic Thai-style fried rice on page 46, but uses fresh thick flat rice noodles instead of leftover rice. It is best served straight from the wok with green coral lettuce leaves and chilli sauce alongside. The smooth sweet chilli sauce will keep for up to 2 weeks in an airtight container in the fridge.

1–2 tablespoons vegetable oil
4 large cloves garlic, finely chopped
10 g Thai salted cabbage (see page 195)
250 g chicken thigh fillets, thinly sliced
2 eggs, lightly beaten
1 tablespoon light soy sauce
1 tablespoon Thai seasoning sauce
  (see page 195)
1 tablespoon oyster sauce
2 teaspoons white sugar
350 g fresh thick flat rice noodles
2 spring onions, cut into 5 cm lengths

freshly ground white pepper
green coral lettuce leaves, to serve

SMOOTH SWEET CHILLI SAUCE
3½ bulbs garlic, peeled
250 g long fresh red chillies
200 ml white vinegar
150 ml water
¼ cup (55 g) white sugar
1 tablespoon salt
1 tablespoon tapioca flour
  (see page 195)

To make the smooth sweet chilli sauce, place all the ingredients in a heavy-based saucepan over low heat and simmer for 20–25 minutes or until the garlic has softened. Remove from the heat and allow to cool to room temperature. Transfer to a blender and blend until smooth, then place in a small bowl and set aside. (Makes about 2 cups.)

Heat the vegetable oil in a wok or large heavy-based frying pan over medium heat. Add the garlic and cabbage and stir-fry for 1–2 minutes. Add the chicken and stir-fry for 3–5 minutes or until the chicken is cooked through. Add the egg and stir for 1 minute or until cooked, then add the soy sauce, seasoning sauce, oyster sauce and sugar. Stir well and add the rice noodles, then cook over high heat for 2–3 minutes, stirring gently to maintain texture and flavour. Add the spring onion and season to taste with white pepper.

Place the stir-fried noodles on a serving platter or large shallow bowl and add the lettuce leaves to the side, then serve with the smooth sweet chilli sauce.

SEN YAI PAD SEE IEW GAI
STIR-FRIED RICE NOODLES WITH SWEET SOY SAUCE & CHICKEN

SERVES 4 AS PART OF A SHARED MEAL

This favourite noodle dish has a strong Chinese influence as most of the ingredients are commonly used in Chinese cooking. However, in Thailand, it is important that the cook achieves the right balance between the garlic and white pepper so as not to overwhelm the other ingredients.

4 large cloves garlic, roughly chopped
1 teaspoon soybean paste (see page 195)
¼ cup (60 ml) vegetable oil
300 g chicken breast fillet, thinly sliced on the diagonal
350 g fresh thick flat rice noodles
1 tablespoon light soy sauce
1 tablespoon Thai seasoning sauce (see page 195)
1 teaspoon white sugar

2 eggs, lightly beaten
150 g (about 3 stems) Chinese broccoli (gai lan), cut into 4–5 cm lengths
½ teaspoon freshly ground white pepper
thinly sliced small red chilli, to serve

PICKLED CHILLI IN VINEGAR
½ cup (125 ml) white vinegar
2 fresh large red chillies, thinly sliced on the diagonal

For the pickled chilli vinegar, place the vinegar and chilli in a bowl and stir to combine. Set aside for 20 minutes before serving.

Place the garlic and soybean paste in a mortar and use the pestle to crush to a coarse paste.

Heat the vegetable oil in a wok or large heavy-based frying pan over medium heat and add the garlic paste, then stir for 1 minute. Add the chicken and stir-fry for 4–5 minutes or until cooked through, then add the noodles and stir quickly. Add the soy sauce, seasoning sauce and sugar and cook, stirring gently, for 2–3 minutes.

Carefully move the noodle mixture to one side of the wok or pan, add the beaten egg to the other side and stir well, then fold the noodles on top of the egg. When the egg is cooked, add the Chinese broccoli and white pepper and stir for 1 minute or until the broccoli is just tender, then remove from the heat. Scatter with sliced chilli.

Serve the noodles with the pickled chilli slices scattered over the top.

PED PHA LHO
DUCK NOODLE SOUP

SERVES 6

When I think of Thai comfort food, this warming noodle soup fits the bill. Right across Thailand you will find people enjoying this fragrant soup from a street-food vendor at any time of the day – or night – as it is a great source of protein and carbohydrate in the one bowl. Although it is cooked the Chinese way, the addition of the super-hot seasoning vinegar makes it very Thai.

4 coriander roots, well washed and crushed
1 × 70 g piece galangal (see page 194), sliced
12 large cloves garlic, crushed
6 duck marylands
3 pandan leaves (see page 195)
1 tablespoon black peppercorns, crushed
5 sticks cinnamon
10 star anise
⅓ cup (90 g) soft palm sugar
½ cup (125 ml) light soy sauce

1 tablespoon dark soy sauce
2 tablespoons Thai seasoning sauce (see page 195)
100 ml oyster sauce
2 litres water
100 g dried thin rice noodles
100 g (about 3 stems) Chinese broccoli (gai lan), trimmed and cut into 4–5 cm lengths
Seasoning Vinegar (see page 191), to serve

Place the coriander roots, galangal and garlic in a large, deep heavy-based saucepan or stockpot and add the duck, pandan leaves, pepper, cinnamon, star anise, palm sugar, soy sauces, seasoning sauce, oyster sauce and water. Bring to the boil over medium heat, then reduce the heat to low and simmer, covered, for at least 2 hours or until the duck is tender.

Meanwhile, place the noodles in a large bowl and cover with cold water, then leave to soak for 1 hour. Drain.

Blanch the Chinese broccoli in a saucepan of boiling water for 1 minute, then drain.

To serve, divide the drained noodles and Chinese broccoli evenly among 6 large soup bowls and add a duck maryland to each. Ladle the soup into the bowls and serve with the seasoning vinegar in a small bowl alongside.

STIR-FRIES

HOY PIPIS PAD HO-RA-PHA

STIR-FRIED PIPIS WITH THAI SWEET BASIL

SERVES 6 AS PART OF A SHARED MEAL

This dish is extremely popular in the coastal areas of Thailand. Combining pipis with crushed garlic and Thai sweet basil creates a wonderful aroma that is noticed as soon as the dish lands on the table. Tapioca flour is added to thicken the delicious sauce.

1 kg live pipis
6 large cloves garlic, crushed
7 red birds-eye chillies, crushed
2 teaspoons tapioca flour (see page 195) or rice flour
1 tablespoon oyster sauce
2 tablespoons fish sauce
1 tablespoon white sugar
2 tablespoons Thai seasoning sauce (see page 195)
2½ tablespoons water
2 tablespoons vegetable oil
4 kaffir lime leaves, torn
4-5 sprigs Thai sweet basil (see page 195)
1 large fresh red chilli, sliced on the diagonal

Place the pipis in a bowl of cold water and leave to soak for 1 hour to remove the sand and grit. Lift out the pipis and drain well.

Place the garlic and birds-eye chillies in a mortar and use the pestle to pound to a rough paste. Place the tapioca flour, oyster sauce, fish sauce, sugar, seasoning sauce and water in a small bowl and stir until the sugar has dissolved.

Heat the vegetable oil in a wok or heavy-based frying pan over medium–high heat. Add the garlic paste and stir for 1 minute or until aromatic. Add the pipis and stir well, then cover and cook for 2 minutes. Remove the lid and add the tapioca flour mixture, then stir well. Add the kaffir lime leaves and cook, covered, for 3-4 minutes or until the pipis have opened. Add the Thai basil and sliced chilli. Transfer the pipi mixture to a serving plate or bowl and serve.

GOONG PAD BAI CHA PHLU
STIR-FRIED KING PRAWNS WITH BETEL LEAVES

SERVES 4 AS PART OF A SHARED MEAL

I discovered this divine southern Thai seafood dish when I lived in Phuket with my mother-in-law's family. During this time, I was also introduced to the idea of using fresh turmeric and betel leaf in a stir-fried curry. I enjoy this dish because it is aromatic from the turmeric-based curry paste and smooth, thanks to the touch of coconut cream that is a must to include at the end.

⅓ cup (80 ml) vegetable oil
⅔ cup (100 g) Southern Curry
   Paste (see page 186)
8 very large raw king prawns, peeled and
   deveined, with tails intact
2 tablespoons fish sauce

1½ tablespoons white sugar
50 g (50) betel leaves, cut into
   1 cm-thick slices
100 ml coconut cream
1½ fresh large red chillies, julienned
4 kaffir lime leaves, julienned

Heat the vegetable oil in a wok or heavy-based frying pan over medium heat. Add the curry paste and cook for 30 seconds or until the paste is aromatic, taking care not to burn it.

Add the prawns and stir well. Add the fish sauce and sugar and stir-fry for 2 minutes or until the prawns just change colour. Add half of the betel leaves and stir until wilted, then add coconut cream, half of the chilli and the kaffir lime leaves and toss together well, stir-frying until the prawns are just cooked and the coconut cream is heated through. Transfer the prawn mixture to a serving plate, then scatter with the remaining betel leaves and chilli, then serve.

GOONG PAD CHA

STIR-FRIED KING PRAWNS IN PAD CHA CURRY PASTE

SERVES 4 AS PART OF A SHARED MEAL

The dance of flavours from the herbs in the curry paste, chilli and Thai sweet basil makes this dish very appetising – your senses of smell, taste and sight are all equally involved. The contrasting colours and shapes make this very visually interesting, too.

⅓ cup (80 ml) vegetable oil
⅔ cup (130 g) *Pad Cha* Curry
 Paste (see page 184)
8 very large raw king prawns, peeled
 and deveined, with tails intact
1 tablespoon fish sauce
1 tablespoon Thai seasoning
 sauce (see page 195)
1 tablespoon white sugar

2 apple eggplants (aubergines)
 (see page 194), cut into wedges
40 g (25–30) pea eggplants (aubergines)
 (see page 195)
4 kaffir lime leaves, torn
1 fresh large green chilli, thinly sliced
1 fresh large red chilli, thinly sliced
5 sprigs Thai sweet basil
 (see page 195)

Heat the vegetable oil in a wok or heavy-based frying pan over medium heat. Add the curry paste and stir for 2–3 minutes or until the paste is aromatic, taking care not to burn it. Add the prawns and stir well, then add the fish sauce, seasoning sauce and sugar and stir well. If the paste is too dry, add 50–100 ml water, then add the apple and pea eggplants and stir. Add the kaffir lime leaves and half of the green and red chilli and stir well. Stir-fry for 2 minutes or until the prawns are just cooked, then add half of the basil sprigs.

Transfer the prawn mixture to a serving plate, then scatter with the remaining chilli and basil and serve.

PLA PAD KHING

STIR-FRIED SNAPPER FILLETS WITH GINGER

SERVES 4-6 AS PART OF A SHARED MEAL

The Chinese influence in this dish is strong, but over time it has been adapted to suit the Thai palate by adding soybean paste and Thai seasoning sauce. Thais enjoy the texture and strong gingery flavour, as a lot of young ginger is used to make up the vegetable component. The saltiness comes from the soy sauce. Other meat such as pork, chicken or seafood may be used, or you can omit the fish to make this vegetarian.

¼ cup (40 g) tapioca flour (see page 195)

1 tablespoon rice flour

400 g snapper fillets, skin removed, pin-boned and cut into bite-sized pieces

2 cups (500 ml) vegetable oil, plus extra for stir-frying

6 large cloves garlic, crushed

2 tablespoons soybean paste (see page 195)

1 tablespoon Thai seasoning sauce (see page 195)

1 tablespoon light soy sauce

¼ cup (55 g) white sugar

¼ cup (60 ml) water

200 g fresh young ginger, peeled and julienned

1½ fresh large red chillies, thinly sliced (optional)

2 spring onions, cut into 5 cm lengths

1 stalk Chinese celery (see page 194), cut into 5 cm lengths, a few leaves reserved for garnish

30 g fresh black fungus (cloud ear or wood fungus), cut into 1 cm lengths or 5 g dried black fungus, soaked in cold water for 30 minutes, well drained and thinly sliced

Combine the tapioca flour and rice flour on a plate. Coat both sides of the fish in the flour mixture, then shake to remove the excess.

Heat the vegetable oil in a deep-fryer or large heavy-based saucepan until it reaches 165°C on a sugar/deep-fry thermometer. Working in batches if necessary to avoid crowding the pan, add the snapper and deep-fry for 3–4 minutes or until just cooked through. Remove the fish and drain on paper towel.

Place the garlic and soybean paste in a mortar and pound with the pestle to a coarse paste.

Heat 2 tablespoons vegetable oil in a wok or heavy-based frying pan over medium heat. Add the garlic mixture and stir for 30 seconds or until aromatic, taking care not to burn. Add the snapper, seasoning sauce, soy sauce, sugar and water and stir well. Add the ginger and chilli, if using, and stir-fry until the ginger is tender. Add the spring onion, celery and black fungus and stir-fry for 1 minute or until slightly softened. Remove from the heat and serve, scattered with the reserved celery leaves.

PAD PRIK KHING PLA

STIR-FRIED CRISPY FISH FILLET WITH RED CURRY PASTE

SERVES 4-6 AS PART OF A SHARED MEAL

When I was young, my mother cooked this dish with freshwater catfish caught from a pond in our paddy fields. Mum cut the fish into cutlets, then deep-fried it and broke it into bite-sized pieces. The final touch was to stir-fry the fish with red curry paste enriched with kaffir lime rind and leaf, palm sugar and fish sauce. In Australia, I use snapper, otherwise this is the same as how Mum used to make it.

500 g snapper fillets, skin removed,
   pin-boned and cut into 5 cm-thick slices
¼ cup (35 g) tapioca flour (see page 195)
2¼ cups (560 ml) vegetable oil
⅔ cup (150 g) Red Curry Paste
   (see page 184)
150 g green beans, topped and cut into
   5 cm lengths

1 tablespoon fish sauce
2 tablespoons soft palm sugar
5 kaffir lime leaves, torn, plus 3 julienned
1½ large fresh red chillies, thinly sliced
   on the diagonal

Dust the fish on both sides with tapioca flour, shaking off the excess. Heat the vegetable oil in a deep-fryer or large heavy-based saucepan until it reaches 180°C on a sugar/deep-fry thermometer. Working in batches if necessary to avoid crowding the pan, deep-fry the fish for 8 minutes or until pale golden and just cooked through. Drain the fish on paper towel.

Heat the remaining ¼ cup (60 ml) oil in a wok or large heavy-based frying pan over medium heat. Add the curry paste and stir for 2–3 minutes or until aromatic, then add the beans, fish sauce and palm sugar and stir well. Add the fish and torn kaffir lime leaves and cook for 3 minutes or until the fish is heated through. Scatter with the chilli and julienned kaffir lime leaves. Transfer the fish mixture to a serving bowl and serve.

KRA PRAO GAI SAP
BASIL MINCED CHICKEN

SERVES 4 AS PART OF A SHARED MEAL

Kra prao is Thai for holy basil or hot basil, and this dish, featuring this fragrant herb, is cooked often in most households in Thailand. While there are many small differences in the cooking method, all versions combine holy basil, garlic and fresh chilli. I also enjoy another rendition of this, which includes pickled bamboo and sliced, rather than minced, chicken (*pad kra prao gai*). Try to find holy basil if you can, because if you use other types of basil, the dish just won't be the same.

190 ml vegetable oil
6–7 sprigs holy basil (see page 194)
6 large cloves garlic, crushed
6 birds-eye chillies, finely chopped
400 g chicken thigh fillets, minced
2 tablespoons dark soy sauce
1 tablespoon fish sauce

1 tablespoon Thai seasoning sauce
  (see page 195)
1 tablespoon white sugar
1 large fresh red chilli, sliced on
  the diagonal
1 large fresh green chilli, sliced on
  the diagonal

Pour 150 ml of the vegetable oil into a small heavy-based saucepan and heat over medium heat. When the oil is hot, add 2 sprigs of the holy basil and deep-fry for 10–20 seconds or until crisp. Remove with a slotted spoon and transfer to paper towel to drain.

Heat the remaining 2 tablespoons oil in a wok or heavy-based frying pan over medium heat. Add the garlic and birds-eye chilli and stir-fry briefly, then add the minced chicken and stir well. Add the dark soy sauce, fish sauce, seasoning sauce and sugar and continue to stir-fry for 4 minutes or until the chicken is cooked and the liquid has almost evaporated. Add the sliced red and green chillies and remaining holy basil sprigs and toss gently to combine. Remove from the heat. Garnish with the fried basil leaves and serve.

STIR-FRIED CHICKEN WITH LEMONGRASS

SERVES 4 AS PART OF A SHARED MEAL

This fragrant dish includes a lemongrass paste base that is prepared first. As this paste has no chilli, large red chillies are used as a vegetable to add a little kick to the dish – you can omit them if you prefer. Seafood such as prawns can be used instead of chicken, to great effect.

2 tablespoons vegetable oil
400 g chicken breast fillet, thinly sliced
   on the diagonal
2 teaspoons fish sauce
2 teaspoons Thai seasoning sauce
   (see page 195)
1 teaspoon white sugar
¼ cup (60 ml) water
2 red shallots, quartered and sliced

½ stick lemongrass, very thinly sliced
1 large fresh red chilli, thinly sliced
   on the diagonal
4 kaffir lime leaves, torn

LEMONGRASS PASTE
½ stick lemongrass, very thinly sliced
1 large red shallot, thinly sliced
6 large cloves garlic, thinly sliced

For the lemongrass paste, place the lemongrass, shallot and garlic in a mortar and use the pestle to pound to a coarse paste.

Heat the vegetable oil in a wok or heavy-based frying pan over medium heat, then add the lemongrass paste and stir for 1–2 minutes or until aromatic. Add the chicken and stir well. Add the fish sauce, seasoning sauce, sugar and the water and simmer for 3–4 minutes or until the chicken is cooked through. Add the shallot, lemongrass and three-quarters each of the sliced chilli and kaffir lime leaves. Stir well, then transfer to a serving plate. Scatter with the remaining chilli and kaffir lime leaves and serve.

KRA PRAO GAI KROB

STIR-FRIED CRISPY CHICKEN WITH BASIL

SERVES 4 AS PART OF A SHARED MEAL

Here, the fried coated chicken becomes crispy and absorbs more flavour from the basil-infused sauce. The high heat at the end of cooking makes the sugar adhere to the crispy chicken, giving it a lovely caramelised finish. You could use beef, prawn or crispy pork belly (see page 176) instead of chicken.

¼ cup (35 g) tapioca flour (see page 195)
1 tablespoon rice flour
400 g chicken breast fillet, thinly sliced
   on the diagonal
vegetable oil, for deep-frying and cooking
6–7 sprigs holy basil (see page 194),
   leaves picked
7 cloves garlic, crushed
5 red birds-eye chillies, finely chopped

100 ml water
1 tablespoon fish sauce
1 tablespoon Thai seasoning
   sauce (see page 195)
1 teaspoon dark soy sauce
1 large fresh red chilli, thinly sliced
   on the diagonal
1 large fresh green chilli, thinly sliced
   on the diagonal

Combine the tapioca flour and rice flour on a plate. Coat the chicken on both sides with the flour mixture and dust off the excess.

Heat vegetable oil for deep-frying in a deep-fryer or large heavy-based saucepan until it reaches 180°C on a sugar/deep-fry thermometer. Working in batches, add the chicken pieces and deep-fry, turning, for 4 minutes or until golden and cooked through. Remove the chicken and drain on paper towel.

Deep-fry one-third of the basil leaves in the hot oil for 10–15 seconds or until crisp, then remove and drain on paper towel.

Heat 2 tablespoons vegetable oil in a wok or heavy-based frying pan over medium heat. Add the garlic and birds-eye chillies and stir until aromatic. Add the water, fish sauce, seasoning sauce, dark soy sauce and sliced red and green chillies. Bring to the boil, then reduce the heat to low and simmer for 2 minutes. Add the chicken and remaining holy basil leaves and toss until heated through.

Transfer the chicken mixture to a serving bowl. Scatter with the fried basil leaves and serve.

GAI PAD MED MA MUANG
STIR-FRIED CHICKEN WITH CASHEWS

SERVES 4 AS PART OF A SHARED MEAL

Stir-fries featuring cashews have long been one of the most enjoyable dishes in Thai cuisine and they are still popular today. The complexity of flavours in this dish, based on my homemade chilli jam, makes it really interesting. Cashews are often added to chicken stir-fries, but you can use any meat of your choice – the king of the dish is still the cashew.

¾ cup (100 g) unsalted cashews

2 tablespoons vegetable oil

6 large cloves garlic, crushed

400 g chicken breast fillet, thinly sliced on the diagonal

1 tablespoon Chilli Jam (see page 188)

1 tablespoon light soy sauce

2 tablespoons Thai oyster sauce

2½ tablespoons water

2 tablespoons white sugar

1 small onion, halved and thinly sliced

1 large fresh red chilli, thinly sliced on the diagonal

1 large fresh green chilli, thinly sliced on the diagonal

2 spring onions, cut into 5 cm lengths

Heat a dry wok or heavy-based frying pan over medium heat, then stir-fry the cashews for 1 minute. Transfer the cashews to a bowl and set aside.

Heat the vegetable oil in the wok or frying pan over medium heat. Add the garlic and cook for 1 minute, then add the chicken, chilli jam and soy sauce and stir well. Add the oyster sauce, water and sugar and stir-fry for 3–4 minutes or until the chicken is cooked through. Add the onion, chillies and three-quarters of the cashews and cook for a further minute. Add three-quarters of the spring onion and stir-fry until just softened. Scatter with the remaining cashews and spring onion and serve.

KRA PRAO MOO KROB
STIR-FRIED CRISPY PORK BELLY WITH BASIL

SERVES 4 AS PART OF A SHARED MEAL

This is one of the most frequently ordered dishes at Spice I Am, so I am sharing my secrets of how to make it with you. What makes it really special is the way the fried pork belly absorbs the sauce, yet still retains its crispness, making it the perfect accompaniment for steamed rice. The blend of sweet and salty, plus the kick from the hot chilli is outstanding, and will make you come back for more.

vegetable oil, for deep-frying and cooking
6–7 sprigs holy basil (see page 194),
   leaves picked
6 large cloves garlic, thinly sliced
6 birds-eye chillies, thinly sliced
¼ cup (60 ml) water
1 tablespoon fish sauce

1 tablespoon Thai seasoning sauce
   (see page 195)
2 teaspoons dark soy sauce
1 tablespoon white sugar
2 large fresh red chillies, julienned
300 g Crispy Pork Belly (see page 176)

Heat vegetable oil for deep-frying in a deep-fryer or deep heavy-based saucepan until it reaches 170°C on a sugar/deep-fry thermometer. Deep-fry one-third of the holy basil leaves for 10–15 seconds or until crisp, then drain on paper towel.

Place the garlic and birds-eye chillies in a mortar and pound with the pestle until well crushed.

Heat 2 tablespoons vegetable oil in a wok or heavy-based frying pan over high heat. Add the garlic paste and stir-fry for 2 minutes or until aromatic. Add the water (taking care as the mixture will spit), fish sauce, seasoning sauce, dark soy sauce and sugar and stir well. Add the julienned chilli and bring to the boil. Add the pork belly and remaining holy basil leaves and stir quickly until the pork is heated through. Scatter with the fried basil leaves and serve.

MOO KROB PAD PRIK PAO
STIR-FRIED CRISPY PORK BELLY WITH CHILLI JAM

SERVES 4 AS PART OF A SHARED MEAL

Here's one of my family's favourite dishes that my mother often cooked for us
– thanks Mum! In Thailand, when cooking oil wasn't widely available, Mum was
always proud of how she made her own cooking oil from pork lard, then used
the crispy leftover bits to make another dish by adding a few vegetables and
her own chilli jam.

4 large cloves garlic, crushed
3 red birds-eye chillies, crushed
2 tablespoons vegetable oil
2 tablespoons Chilli Jam (see page 188)
100 ml water
1 tablespoon fish sauce
2 tablespoons white sugar

5 cherry tomatoes, halved
2 spring onions, cut into 5 cm lengths,
 plus extra julienned for garnishing
300 g Crispy Pork Belly (see page 176)
1 large fresh red chilli, thinly sliced
 on the diagonal

Place the garlic and birds-eye chillies in a mortar and pound with the pestle to
a coarse paste.

Heat the vegetable oil in a wok or heavy-based frying pan over medium heat.
Add the garlic paste and cook for 30 seconds or until aromatic, taking care not
to burn it. Add the chilli jam and stir well. Carefully add the water, fish sauce,
sugar and cherry tomato and stir. Add the spring onion and stir, then add the
pork belly and chilli and stir-fry until the pork is heated through.

Transfer the pork mixture to a serving dish, then scatter with the julienned spring
onion and serve.

SALADS

SOM TUM

GREEN PAPAYA SALAD WITH DRIED SHRIMP, PEANUT & CHILLI

SERVES 4 AS PART OF A SHARED MEAL

This refreshing, light salad is made by pounding the ingredients with a mortar and pestle. However, be careful not to over-pound, crush or grind them or the texture will be too smooth; the salad needs to be a little textured. The papaya needs to be completely firm – you can buy them from Asian grocery stores in this unripe state.

1 clove garlic, peeled
1 large fresh red chilli, crushed
15 g dried shrimp (see page 194)
40 g long green beans, cut into
   3 cm lengths
30 g roasted unsalted peanuts

1 tablespoon soft palm sugar
1½ tablespoons lime juice
1½ tablespoons fish sauce
4 cherry tomatoes, halved
100 g green papaya flesh, julienned
thinly sliced lime, to serve

Place the garlic and chilli in a mortar and use the pestle to crush. Add the shrimp and long beans and pound a few times to bruise the beans. Add the peanuts and pound a few more times. Add the palm sugar and lightly grind until it has dissolved, then add the lime juice and fish sauce. Add the cherry tomato and lightly crush. Add the papaya and softly pound, then mix well with a spoon.

Serve with a lime slice on top.

YUM THA KRAI
CRISPY PRAWN & LEMONGRASS SALAD

SERVES 4 AS PART OF A SHARED MEAL

Prawns and lemongrass are a heavenly match – just be sure to take the time to finely slice the lemongrass or it won't be that nice to eat. The fragrant, citrus flavour of lemongrass also goes well with other seafood, so you could use fish instead of the prawns, if you prefer.

6 large raw king prawns, peeled and
    deveined, with tails intact
50 g tapioca flour (see page 195)
2 cups (500 ml) vegetable oil
50 g unsalted cashews, toasted
1 large stick lemongrass, very thinly sliced
2 red shallots, halved and thinly sliced
1½ spring onions, julienned
small handful coriander leaves
4 sprigs roundleaf mint (see page 195),
    leaves picked

1 large fresh red chilli, julienned
roasted cashews (optional), to serve

DRESSING
3 large cloves garlic, peeled
3 fresh red birds-eye chillies, sliced
2 tablespoons soft palm sugar
70 ml fish sauce
50 ml lime juice

For the dressing, place the garlic and chillies in a mortar and use the pestle to lightly crush. Add the palm sugar, fish sauce and lime juice and stir to mix well until the sugar has dissolved. Set aside.

Coat the prawns in tapioca flour and dust off any excess. Heat the vegetable oil in a heavy-based saucepan over high heat until hot. Add the prawns and deep-fry for 2–3 minutes or until they change colour and are just cooked through. Remove with a slotted spoon and drain on paper towel.

Roughly crush the cashews with the mortar and pestle and transfer to a small bowl. Add the lemongrass, shallot, spring onion, coriander, mint and chilli to the bowl of crushed cashews and toss gently to mix. Reserve 1 tablespoon of the dressing and pour the remainder over the lemongrass salad, then toss again.

Place the prawns and salad on a serving plate, then scatter with the roasted cashews, if using. Drizzle with the reserved dressing and serve.

YUM HUA PLEE
BANANA FLOWER SALAD

SERVES 4 AS PART OF A SHARED MEAL

This textural, fragrant salad is always a hit when it reaches the table. It is still a family favourite – I remember when I was a kid we'd gather the banana flowers from the garden for Mum to prepare for us. It was always a treat. I like to serve this on a banana flower petal.

100 g minced chicken
200 ml coconut cream
150 g banana flower heart, julienned
¼ cup (20 g) shredded coconut, toasted
40 g Fried Red Shallots (see page 179)
1 tablespoon Chilli Jam (see page 188)

1 tablespoon grated palm sugar
1 tablespoon fish sauce
1 tablespoon tamarind puree (see page 195)
1 spring onion, julienned
julienned large fresh red chilli, to serve

Combine the chicken and half of the coconut cream in a small heavy-based saucepan, then stir over medium heat for 4–5 minutes or until the chicken is cooked through. Remove the pan from the heat and leave the chicken mixture to cool to room temperature.

Add the remaining coconut cream to the pan and stir to mix well, then transfer the chicken mixture to a bowl. Add the banana flower heart, toasted coconut and shallot and toss to combine.

Place the chilli jam, palm sugar, fish sauce and tamarind puree in a small bowl, then stir until the sugar has dissolved. Add three-quarters of the spring onion to the chicken mixture and toss well.

Drizzle most of the dressing over the salad, then transfer the salad to a plate. Scatter over the remaining spring onion and the julienned chilli, then drizzle with the remaining dressing and serve.

YUM WOON SEN GAI SAB

MUNG BEAN VERMICELLI SALAD WITH CHICKEN

SERVES 4 AS PART OF A SHARED MEAL

I love this healthy salad, as it is just bursting with fresh flavours and contrasting textures. Although it is best served just after it is made, if you want to prepare it in advance and serve it chilled, then you'll need to add more dressing as the noodles soak it up. Seafood works well instead of chicken – try chopped fish fillets or small prawns.

40 g minced chicken
40 g raw unsalted peanuts
100 g mung bean vermicelli
60 g dried shrimp (see page 194)
1 spring onion, thinly sliced
small handful coriander, sliced,
  plus extra to garnish
1 red shallot, halved and thinly sliced
1 large fresh red chilli, julienned

DRESSING
1 clove garlic, peeled
1–2 small fresh red chillies, crushed
1 coriander root, cleaned
2 tablespoons soft palm sugar
¼ cup (60 ml) fish sauce
¼ cup (60 ml) lime juice

For the dressing, place the garlic, chillies and coriander root in a mortar and use the pestle to pound to a paste. Add the palm sugar and lightly grind until dissolved. Add the fish sauce and lime juice and pound until well combined. Set aside.

Cook the minced chicken in a small saucepan of boiling water for 3 minutes or until cooked through. Drain and set aside.

Lightly dry-roast the peanuts in a dry, small heavy-based frying pan over medium heat until light golden. Set aside.

Place the vermicelli in a heatproof bowl, then cover with boiling water and leave to soak for 2 minutes. Drain well and place in a mixing bowl. Add the dressing, chicken and dried shrimp and mix well, then add the spring onion, coriander, shallot and peanuts and mix well. Scatter with the chilli and extra coriander and serve.

YUM GAI
CHICKEN & LEMONGRASS SALAD

SERVES 8 AS PART OF A SHARED MEAL

Another super-healthy salad, this is light in both texture and flavour. Be sure to use the freshest herbs you can find, and not to overcook the chicken so it stays lovely and tender.

400 g chicken breast fillet
2 cups (500 ml) water
vegetable oil, for deep-frying
120 g unsalted cashews
2 spring onions, julienned
¾ stick lemongrass, very thinly sliced
2 × 4 cm pieces ginger, julienned
4 large fresh red chillies, julienned
20 g (1 small bunch) coriander leaves

DRESSING
3 large cloves garlic, crushed
5 red birds-eye chillies, crushed
2½ tablespoons soft palm sugar
⅓ cup (80 ml) fish sauce
¼ cup (60 ml) lime juice

For the dressing, place the garlic, chillies and palm sugar in a mortar and use the pestle to pound to a coarse paste. Stir in the fish sauce and lime juice and set aside.

Place the chicken in a heavy-based saucepan and cover with the water. Bring to the boil over medium heat, then reduce the heat to low and simmer, covered, for 5 minutes. Remove the pan from the heat and leave the chicken to rest in the liquid for 40 minutes to cook completely, then remove, drain well and shred into thin strips.

Meanwhile, heat vegetable oil for deep-frying in a heavy-based saucepan. Add the cashews to the hot oil and deep-fry for 1 minute or until golden brown; watch carefully as they become bitter when overcooked. Remove immediately with a mesh skimmer and leave to drain on paper towel.

Place the chicken in a bowl with the spring onion, lemongrass and three-quarters each of the ginger, chilli and coriander.

Roughly crush two-thirds of the cashews using a mortar and pestle (or with the flat side of a cleaver on a chopping board), then add to the chicken mixture. Pour over three-quarters of the dressing and toss well.

Place the salad on a serving plate and scatter with the remaining cashews. Drizzle with a little more salad dressing and scatter with the remainder of the ginger, chilli and coriander. Serve with the remaining dressing in a bowl to the side.

LARB GAI
MINCED CHICKEN SALAD

SERVES 4 AS PART OF A SHARED MEAL

I like to serve this aromatic chicken salad with loads of crispy green vegetables – try sliced cucumber, lettuce leaves and snowpeas, or whatever raw vegetables you like. Minced snapper, duck, pork or beef also work well with these flavours.

400 g minced chicken
50 ml water
50 ml fish sauce
50 ml lime juice
2 teaspoons chilli powder
3 spring onions, finely chopped
1 red shallot, halved and thinly sliced

2 sprigs coriander, roughly chopped
2 sprigs roundleaf mint (see page 195)
2 sprigs Vietnamese coriander (see page 195), finely chopped
2 tablespoons Ground Roasted Rice (see page 178)

Place the chicken in a small heavy-based saucepan and add the water, then cook over high heat, stirring well to break up the chicken, for 5 minutes or until the chicken is cooked. Remove from the heat and add the fish sauce, lime juice and chilli powder and stir to mix well. Leave to cool a little.

Add the spring onion, shallot, coriander, mint and Vietnamese coriander to the chicken mixture and stir to combine. Add the ground roasted rice, then gently mix. Transfer to a serving bowl and serve.

YUM NUA
CHARGRILLED BEEF SALAD

SERVES 4 AS PART OF A SHARED MEAL

This is probably one of the best-known Thai salads outside Thailand. Its hot and spicy flavours just about dance as you eat it, and the mint adds a distinctive note of freshness.

1 × 200 g beef sirloin or rump steak
½ small lebanese cucumber, thinly sliced
3 cherry tomatoes, halved
1½ spring onions, finely chopped
small handful coriander leaves
1 red shallot, halved and thinly sliced

6–8 sprigs roundleaf mint (see page 195)
⅓ stick lemongrass, very thinly sliced
3 kaffir lime leaves, julienned
1 large fresh red chilli, julienned
1 quantity Beef Salad Dressing
  (see page 192)

Preheat the oven to 160°C (140°C fan-forced).

Heat a chargrill pan over high heat, then cook the beef on both sides until seared. Transfer to a roasting tin and roast for 8–10 minutes for medium–rare, then remove from the oven and leave to rest for 10 minutes.

Slice the beef thinly on the diagonal, then place in a bowl. Add the cucumber, tomato, spring onion, coriander, shallot, mint, lemongrass, kaffir lime leaves and chilli. Transfer to a serving plate.

Spoon the dressing over the beef salad and toss gently to combine, then serve.

CURRIES

HOR MOK PLA

STEAMED FISH CURRY IN BANANA LEAVES

MAKES 10–12 (SERVES 6 AS PART OF A SHARED MEAL)

Hor mok means 'wrap and hide' and refers to food wrapped in banana leaves that is then steamed. Here, I've used fish, but you can also cook chicken or seafood in this way. In some areas of Thailand, this dish is prepared without coconut cream and may include different herbs and spices. The fragrant fish mixture may be cooked in an open basket made from banana leaves, as in the recipe below, or in ramekins, although the water from the steam may reduce the intensity of the flavour. For those with more skill, portions of the mixture can be completely folded into banana leaf 'pyramids' (see opposite), which is how we serve this at the restaurant. If the banana leaves are very mature, blanch them quickly in a saucepan of boiling water or wave them briefly over a gas flame to make them pliable before adding the filling.

1 egg, lightly beaten

2 tablespoons fish sauce

100 g Red Curry Paste (see page 184)

2 cups (500 ml) coconut cream, plus extra to garnish

500 g snapper or basa fillets, skin removed and pin-boned

1 tablespoon vegetable oil

2 large young banana leaves

24 betel leaves

3 kaffir lime leaves, julienned

¾ large fresh red chilli, julienned

Place the egg, fish sauce and red curry paste in a large bowl and stir until well combined. Add the coconut cream and stir until combined.

Thinly slice 250 g of the fish fillets and mince the remainder in a food processor, pulsing and taking care not to over-process. Add all of the fish and the oil to the egg mixture and stir gently for 3–4 minutes until very well mixed.

Cut the banana leaves into ten 17 cm-diameter rounds (or twelve 15 cm-diameter rounds). Place a banana leaf round on a work surface, shiny side down, and place a few torn betel leaves in the centre. At 4 evenly spaced intervals, crimp the leaf to form a 'basket', securing each pleat with a small toothpick. Add 2–3 tablespoons of the fish mixture to the banana leaf basket, then top with some julienned kaffir lime leaves and chilli. Drizzle a little extra coconut cream over the fish. Repeat with the remaining banana leaf rounds, betel leaves, fish mixture, kaffir lime leaves and chilli.

Place a steamer basket over a wok or large heavy-based saucepan of simmering water. Working in batches, place the banana baskets in a single layer in the steamer and steam over high heat for 10–15 minutes or until the fish mixture is cooked, then serve.

GAENG SOM GOONG
CLEAR SWEET & SOUR PRAWN CURRY

SERVES 6 AS PART OF A SHARED MEAL

Popular in central Thailand, this easy style of curry gets its distinctive sour flavour from the addition of tamarind. You can add many different vegetables, depending on what is in season. It is one of the dishes I miss when I'm away from home as it is one of my mother's favourites and she cooked it often when we were kids – we all still look forward to it. You may use other types of seafood with a firm texture such as mudfish or snapper fillets. This recipe is best made a day ahead and stored in the fridge to allow the flavours to develop, then reheated just before serving.

300 g long melon (see page 194), peeled and cut into bite-sized pieces
150 g Sour Curry Paste (see page 183)
3 cups (750 ml) water
1 cup (250 ml) tamarind puree (see page 195)
⅓ cup (80 ml) fish sauce
1 teaspoon salt
150 g soft palm sugar

200 g water spinach (morning glory), trimmed and cut into 5 cm lengths
200 g choy sum, trimmed and cut into 5 cm lengths
100 g oyster mushrooms, roughly torn
8 large raw king prawns, peeled and deveined, with tails intact
3 kaffir lime leaves, torn

Combine the long melon, sour curry paste and water in a large heavy-based saucepan or wok and bring to the boil over medium heat. Reduce the heat to low and simmer for 2 minutes. Add the tamarind puree, fish sauce, salt and palm sugar and bring back to the boil. Add the water spinach, choy sum and oyster mushrooms and simmer for 1–2 minutes, then add the prawns and simmer for 2 minutes or until the prawns have changed colour and are just cooked. Add the kaffir lime leaves and stir, then remove from the heat and serve.

GAENG PLA BAI CHA PRU
SOUTHERN-STYLE FISH CURRY WITH BETEL LEAVES

SERVES 6 AS PART OF A SHARED MEAL

I first tried this fantastic curry when I lived in Phuket, and it is one of the best dishes from southern Thailand I've ever tasted. The curry paste includes turmeric, which not only gives it colour, but adds an earthy flavour that matches the meatiness of the blue-eye trevalla perfectly. When this hits the table, steam from the curry tickles your nose as the aroma spreads throughout the room. While this is good served with steamed rice, I prefer it with vermicelli noodles alongside.

¼ cup (60 ml) vegetable oil
200 g Southern Curry Paste (see page 186)
500 g blue-eye trevalla fillets, skin on and thickly sliced
¼ cup (60 ml) fish sauce
½ teaspoon white sugar

4 kaffir lime leaves, torn
1½ large fresh red chillies, thinly sliced on the diagonal
1 × 400 ml tin coconut milk
30 betel leaves, torn

Heat the vegetable oil in a heavy-based saucepan over medium heat. Add the curry paste and stir for 2 minutes or until it is aromatic. Add the fish and stir gently for 1 minute. Add the fish sauce, sugar, kaffir lime leaves and chilli and stir. Add the coconut milk and bring to the boil, then reduce the heat to low and simmer for 3 minutes or until the fish is just cooked through. Add the betel leaves and stir gently, then remove from the heat and serve.

CHOO CHEE PIK YUAK YAD SAI
STUFFED BANANA CHILLIES WITH CHOO CHEE CURRY

SERVES 12 AS PART OF A SHARED MEAL

Choo chee is a sweet, thick and creamy coconut-based curry that is highly aromatic due to the generous amount of red curry paste. Banana chilli is one of the sweetest chillies and is often used as a vegetable in Thailand, as I've done here. You can use a mix of colours of banana chillies, if you can find them.

3 large cloves garlic
10–12 coriander roots, well washed
¼ cup (60 ml) fish sauce
300 g minced chicken
300 g minced raw prawn meat
6 large green banana chillies
 (banana peppers)

70 ml vegetable oil
⅔ cup (150 g) Red Curry Paste
 (see page 184)
2 tablespoons soft palm sugar
1½ large fresh red chillies, julienned
1 small kaffir lime leaf, julienned
300 ml coconut cream

Place the garlic and coriander roots in a mortar and use the pestle to pound to a coarse paste. Add 1 teaspoon of the fish sauce and stir well, then transfer to a mixing bowl. Add the chicken and prawn meat and stir to combine well.

Remove the tops from the banana chillies and scoop out the seeds. Stuff the chillies with the chicken and prawn mixture.

Place a steamer basket over a large heavy-based saucepan of simmering water. Place the stuffed chillies in the steamer and steam, covered, for 12–15 minutes or until the chillies are tender and the stuffing is cooked. Transfer the stuffed chillies to a serving platter and set aside.

Heat the vegetable oil in a heavy-based saucepan over medium heat. Add the curry paste and stir for 2–3 minutes or until aromatic. Add the remaining fish sauce and palm sugar and stir well. Add half of the julienned chilli and kaffir lime leaf, then add the coconut cream. Stir the mixture gently until it is simmering, then remove from the heat. Cut the stuffed chillies into 3–4 cm thick pieces, if you like. Spoon the sauce over the stuffed chillies and garnish with the remaining julienned chilli and kaffir lime leaf, then serve.

GAENG GAI NOR MAI DONG
RED CHICKEN CURRY WITH SOUR BAMBOO

SERVES 6-8 AS PART OF A SHARED MEAL

During the rainy season in Thailand there is always plenty of fresh bamboo growing, so when I was a child, my family would pickle it for storage to see us through the year. The fermentation process gives the bamboo a strong character; however, when cooked in this dish it creates a beautiful result, especially when served with hot steamed rice. In Australia, I use the sliced sour bamboo sold in jars in Asian food stores. This recipe is best made one day ahead and stored in the fridge to allow the flavours to develop, then reheated just before serving.

70 ml vegetable oil

200 g Red Curry Paste (see page 184)

500 g chicken thigh fillets, thinly sliced on the diagonal

¼ cup (60 ml) fish sauce

2 tablespoons soft palm sugar

300 g sliced sour bamboo (available in jars from Asian food stores), rinsed

120 g fresh coconut flesh, cut into 2 cm-thick slices

½ cup (125 ml) fresh coconut juice (also known as coconut water)

2 cups (500 ml) coconut milk

1½ large fresh red chillies, thinly sliced on the diagonal

4 kaffir lime leaves, torn

6 sprigs holy basil (see page 194)

Heat the vegetable oil in a heavy-based saucepan over medium heat. Add the red curry paste and stir for 2 minutes or until it is aromatic. Add the chicken and stir for 2 minutes. Add the fish sauce and palm sugar and stir to combine. Add the bamboo, coconut flesh, coconut juice and coconut milk and stir gently, then cook over medium heat for another 3–4 minutes until the chicken is tender and cooked through. Add the chilli, kaffir lime and basil and stir well, then remove from the heat. Transfer to a serving bowl and serve.

GAENG KA REE
MILD CHICKEN, POTATO & COCONUT MILK CURRY

SERVES 4 AS PART OF A SHARED MEAL

One of the mildest curries in Thai cuisine, this is rich in flavour, aromatic with spices, and sweet due to the smoothness of the coconut cream. I have used thigh fillets here, but you could use 500 g thigh cutlets cut in half through the bone, or drumsticks if you prefer. The curry tastes even better when left to mature in the fridge overnight and then reheated just before serving. As the curry has some influence from Malay cuisine it is quite thick, so it may be eaten with steamed rice or flatbread for dipping into the sauce. It is often accompanied by crisp raw vegetables such as sliced cucumber.

¼ cup (60 ml) vegetable oil
⅔ cup (200 g) Yellow Curry Paste
    (see page 183)
500 g chicken thigh fillets,
    sliced on the diagonal
¼ cup (60 ml) fish sauce

1½ tablespoons soft palm sugar
1 tablespoon tamarind puree (see page 195)
300 g kipfler potatoes, peeled and cut into
    pieces the same size as the chicken
2 red shallots, halved or quartered
2 cups (500 ml) coconut milk

Heat the vegetable oil in a heavy-based saucepan over medium heat until hot. Add the curry paste and stir for 2 minutes or until it is aromatic. Add the chicken and stir for 1–2 minutes, then add the fish sauce, palm sugar, tamarind puree, potato and shallot and stir well.

Reduce the heat to low and cook, stirring often, for 20 minutes or until the potato is almost tender. Add the coconut milk and simmer for a further 10 minutes, without stirring, until the chicken and potato are cooked through. Transfer to a serving bowl and serve.

GAENG AORM GAI
CHICKEN CURRY WITH PUMPKIN & DILL

SERVES 8 AS PART OF A SHARED MEAL

This pungent curry from north-east Thailand has a Lao influence. It reflects the Lao heritage of many of the people in the border provinces, where they speak the same dialect and have the same way of living and female dress code for religious days as their neighbours. This recipe is prepared from ingredients commonly found in a home garden or paddy field in Thailand, and traditionally would include freshwater fish or frog – whatever could be obtained locally and in season. Here I've used chicken instead. If lemon basil is not available, then substitute with additional dill.

1 litre chicken stock
30 g Issan Curry Paste (see page 184)
500 g chicken thigh fillets, cut into 2 cm-thick slices
200 g Kent pumpkin (squash), seeded and cut into bite-sized pieces
2 tablespoons fish sauce
1 tablespoon fermented fish sauce (see page 194)
2 apple eggplants (aubergines) (see page 194), cut into quarters

1 bunch (about 150 g) choy sum, trimmed and cut into 5 cm lengths
large handful dill, chopped
6–7 sprigs lemon basil (see page 194), leaves picked
2 spring onions, cut into lengths
4 red birds-eye chillies, bruised
2 tablespoons Ground Roasted Rice (see page 178)

Place the chicken stock in a large heavy-based saucepan and bring to the boil over medium heat. Add the curry paste and stir to combine. When the stock returns to the boil, add the chicken and pumpkin, then reduce the heat to low and cook for 5–6 minutes or until the chicken and pumpkin are tender and cooked through. Add the fish sauce, fermented fish sauce and apple eggplants and cook for a further 1–2 minutes. Add the choy sum, dill, lemon basil leaves, spring onion, chillies and ground rice and stir well. Cook until the choy sum is just tender, then remove from the heat and serve.

PANANG GAI

PANANG RED CHICKEN CURRY WITH KAFFIR LIME LEAVES

SERVES 4 AS PART OF A SHARED MEAL

A thick curry based on coconut cream and red curry paste, this has a touch of dried spices added to give its signature rich curry character and a lovely smooth, creamy texture that is both sweet, yet salty from the fish sauce. Kaffir lime leaf is an essential ingredient as it adds an aromatic citrus note. You may cook this curry with pork or beef instead of chicken, however they will need to be sliced more thinly to absorb the fragrant flavour of the sauce.

¼ cup (60 ml) vegetable oil
200 g Panang Curry Paste (see page 183)
500 g chicken thigh fillets, thinly sliced
   on the diagonal
¼ cup (60 ml) fish sauce

1 tablespoon soft palm sugar
4 kaffir lime leaves, 3 torn and 1 julienned
1 large fresh red chilli, julienned
200 ml coconut cream

Heat the vegetable oil in a large heavy-based saucepan over medium heat. Add the curry paste and stir for 2 minutes or until it is aromatic. Add the chicken and stir for 2 minutes, then add the fish sauce and palm sugar and stir to combine. Add the torn kaffir lime leaves, three-quarters of the chilli and the coconut cream and stir. Gently bring to a simmer, without stirring, and cook for 3 minutes or until the chicken is tender and cooked through. Transfer to a bowl and garnish with the julienned kaffir lime leaf and remaining chilli and serve.

GAENG PED YANG
ROASTED DUCK RED CURRY WITH EGGPLANT, TOMATO & PINEAPPLE

SERVES 6 AS PART OF A SHARED MEAL

A very popular and sophisticated curry in Thailand, its fine balance of saltiness, sweetness and fruitiness means its popularity has spread around the world. The paste uses a combination of herbs such as lemongrass, galangal and chilli and the sweetness of nutmeg; the rich flavour will really excite your palate. Here, I've served it in a hollowed-out fresh coconut shell. Red duck curry tastes better if left in the fridge overnight to mature before reheating and serving.

¼ cup (60 ml) vegetable oil

200 g Red Duck Curry Paste (see page 180)

500 g roasted duck legs (available from Asian barbecued meat stores), meat removed from the bones and thickly sliced

¼ cup (60 ml) fish sauce

20 pea eggplants (aubergines) (see page 195)

2 apple eggplants (aubergines) (see page 194), cut into quarters

6 tinned lychees, drained, with 2 tablespoons juice reserved

6 cherry tomatoes

1 × 1 cm-thick slice fresh pineapple, peeled and cut into 1 cm dice

⅔ cup (90 g) fresh coconut flesh, thinly sliced

2 teaspoons white sugar

100 ml fresh coconut juice (also known as coconut water)

300 ml coconut milk

1 large fresh red chilli, thinly sliced on the diagonal

5 kaffir lime leaves, torn

5 sprigs Thai sweet basil (see page 195)

Heat the vegetable oil in a large heavy-based saucepan over medium heat. Add the curry paste and stir for 2 minutes or until it is aromatic. Add the duck and stir well. Add the fish sauce, pea eggplants, apple eggplant, lychees, tomatoes, pineapple and coconut flesh and stir until well combined.

Add the sugar, coconut juice, coconut milk and reserved lychee juice, then reduce the heat to low and cook for 5–6 minutes, without stirring, until the duck is heated through. Add the chilli, kaffir lime leaves and sweet basil and stir, then remove from the heat and serve.

GAENG PA NUA
BEEF JUNGLE CURRY

SERVES 8 AS PART OF A SHARED MEAL

This fragrant, brothy curry reminds me of the cooking inspiration I received from my mother's late father. I now use his recipe for this and am proud to share it here. All the paste ingredients came from our backyard, and I remember how my grandfather pounded his own paste and caught his own meat or freshwater fish. Holy basil leaf is used, and holy basil flower is traditionally added to the paste to give it a stronger, hotter flavour. Here, I've used the flowering part of a Thai baby basil stem as a garnish, but regular holy basil leaves can be used if you can't find any flowers. This curry also matches well with fish. In Thailand, jungle curry served with freshly steamed rice is a common dish to sustain people after working hard in the paddies.

3 cups (750 ml) water
⅔ cup (150 g) Jungle Curry
    Paste (see page 186)
2 apple eggplants (aubergines)
    (see page 194), quartered
15 pea eggplants (aubergines)
    (see page 195)
20 g fresh or rinsed and drained pickled
    krachai (see page 194), thinly sliced

4 kaffir lime leaves, torn
¼ cup (60 ml) fish sauce
¼ teaspoon white sugar
1 × 400 g beef eye fillet, thinly sliced
1½ large fresh red chillies, thinly sliced
    on the diagonal
4–5 sprigs holy basil (see page 194)

Bring the water to the boil in a heavy-based saucepan and add the curry paste. Stir and return to a simmer, then add the eggplants, krachai, kaffir lime leaves, fish sauce and sugar. Bring to a simmer again over medium heat, then add the beef and stir gently for 3 minutes or until the beef is just cooked. Transfer to a bowl and garnish with the chilli and holy basil leaves, then serve.

MASSAMAN NUA
SLOW-COOKED MASSAMAN BEEF CURRY WITH POTATO & SHALLOTS

SERVES 6 AS PART OF A SHARED MEAL

It's no surprise that this rich, satisfying, complex curry of coconut cream, palm sugar and sour tamarind puree studded with slow-cooked beef and potatoes is a favourite Thai dish, both within and outside Thailand. It was first recorded in the royal court kitchen during the reign of King Rama II. Although it is best made with beef, as I've done here, it is sometimes cooked with chicken, to great effect.

500 g Slow-cooked Beef (see page 176), cut into bite-sized pieces
1 cup (250 ml) beef stock
1 stick cinnamon
3 star anise
2 cups (500 ml) coconut milk
650 ml coconut cream
¾ cup (150 g) Massaman Curry Paste (see page 180)

400 g kipfler potatoes, peeled and cut into thin rounds
5 red shallots, peeled
1 cup (150 g) roasted unsalted peanuts
1 tablespoon tamarind puree (see page 195)
¼ cup (60 ml) fish sauce
½ teaspoon salt
150 g soft palm sugar

Combine the slow-cooked beef, stock, cinnamon stick, star anise, coconut milk and coconut cream in a heavy-based saucepan and bring to the boil over high heat. Reduce the heat to medium and simmer for 5 minutes. Add the curry paste, potato, shallots, peanuts, tamarind puree, fish sauce, salt and palm sugar and bring to a simmer. Cook over low heat, stirring occasionally, for 20 minutes or until the potato and shallots are tender. Transfer to a serving bowl and serve.

GAENG KEAW WANN NUA TOUN

SLOW-COOKED BEEF & EGGPLANT GREEN CURRY

SERVES 6 AS PART OF A SHARED MEAL

I really enjoy preparing this dish as it involves two processes – the first is cooking the slow-cooked beef and the second is making the fabulous curry sauce. The most exciting part is when the two are combined to create a fantastic dish. This curry is vibrant in colour and the beef has a beautiful soft texture as it absorbs the flavour from the sauce.

¼ cup (60 ml) vegetable oil

200 g Green Curry Paste (see page 180)

500 g Slow-cooked Beef (see page 176), cut into bite-sized pieces

¼ cup (60 ml) fish sauce

2 apple eggplants (aubergines) (see page 194), quartered

15 pea eggplants (aubergines) (see page 195)

10 g fresh or rinsed and drained pickled krachai (see page 194), thinly sliced

2 cups (500 ml) coconut milk

1 teaspoon white sugar

1½ large fresh red chillies, thinly sliced on the diagonal

3 kaffir lime leaves, torn

5 sprigs Thai sweet basil (see page 195)

Heat the vegetable oil in a large heavy-based saucepan over medium heat. Add the curry paste and stir for 2 minutes or until it is aromatic. Add the beef and stir for 1 minute, then add the fish sauce and stir.

Add the eggplants and krachai and stir well. Add the coconut milk, sugar and chilli and stir gently until the mixture comes to the boil. Reduce the heat to low and simmer for 3 minutes or until the beef is heated through and the eggplants are slightly softened, then add the kaffir lime leaves and Thai sweet basil and stir. Transfer to a serving bowl and serve.

KAENG PRIK KA DOOK ORN
SOUTHERN CURRY OF SOFT PORK RIB

SERVES 6 AS PART OF A SHARED MEAL

This is one of the best curries not based on coconut milk from southern Thailand. Rich from the inclusion of cashews and hot from the peppercorns and chilli, its flavour is enhanced by the time taken to cook the soft pork ribs, and by the Thai holy basil added just before serving with steamed rice alongside to sop all the delicious, brothy sauce.

1 × 700 g piece soft pork rib
    (pork forequarter), cut into
    bite-sized pieces
250 g raw unsalted cashews
1 teaspoon salt

2 litres water
100 g Southern Curry Paste (see page 186)
¼ cup (60 ml) fish sauce
5 kaffir lime leaves, torn
4 sprigs Thai holy basil (see page 195)

Place the pork rib, cashews, salt and water in a large heavy-based saucepan and bring to the boil over medium heat. Reduce the heat to very low and simmer for 1 hour, skimming and discarding any fat and impurities from the surface of the stock.

Add the curry paste and stir, then simmer for 4–5 minutes. Add the fish sauce and remove the pan from the heat. Stir in three-quarters each of the kaffir lime leaves and basil. Transfer to a serving bowl and garnish the curry with the remaining kaffir lime leaves and basil, then serve.

FAVOURITES

GOONG MA KHAM
PRAWNS WITH TAMARIND SAUCE

SERVES 4 AS PART OF A SHARED MEAL

Most Thai households have all the seasoning ingredients for this in their kitchen, so they just need to go to the markets and pick up some fresh prawns. The combination of palm sugar, fish sauce and tamarind puree provides the perfect balance of sweet, salty and sour that Thai cuisine strives for. You can also use the tamarind sauce to top a deep-fried whole fish, such as a snapper. The fish flesh absorbs the flavour, providing a nice balance with the crispy skin.

2 cups (500 ml) vegetable oil
8 large raw king prawns, peeled and
   deveined, with tails intact
40 g tapioca flour (see page 195)
20 g rice flour

½ bunch Chinese broccoli (gai lan),
   trimmed and cut into 4–5 cm lengths
300 g Tamarind Sauce (see page 187)
large handful coriander leaves
1 large fresh red chilli, julienned

Heat the vegetable oil in a deep heavy-based saucepan over medium heat. Place the prawns on a large flat plate. Combine the tapioca flour and rice flour and sprinkle over the prawns to coat, then shake off any excess.

Deep-fry a few prawns at a time in the hot oil for 6 minutes or until the prawns just change colour and are cooked through. Remove with a slotted spoon and drain on paper towel. Repeat with the remaining prawns.

Blanch the Chinese broccoli in a saucepan of boiling water for 1–2 minutes, then drain.

Pour the tamarind sauce into a small heavy-based saucepan and bring to the boil over medium heat.

Place the Chinese broccoli on a serving plate and top with the prawns. Drizzle with the hot tamarind sauce and garnish with coriander leaves and chilli, then serve.

PING NGOB
GRILLED FISH CURRY PARCELS

MAKES ABOUT 10

Ngob is a cooking method where ingredients are combined, often with curry paste, then wrapped in banana leaf and grilled over low heat, ideally over a charcoal barbecue. As a boy, I remember my grandfather made the best *ngob*. He caught the freshwater whitebait in the creek near our paddy field, then quickly marinated them with his own special red curry paste. He always cooked with whole foods that were as fresh as possible, so the flavour was natural – this is how I remember his *ping ngob* to this day. Here, I've used ingredients that are easier to find in Australia and have simplified the cooking method to baking in the oven.

500 g silver fish or whitebait
100 g Red Curry Paste (see page 184)
2 eggs, lightly beaten
⅓ cup (50 g) rice flour
¼ cup (60 ml) fish sauce

⅓ cup (50 g) grated fresh coconut flesh
100 ml coconut milk
3 kaffir lime leaves, julienned
4–5 sprigs holy basil (see page 194)
2 banana leaves

Preheat the oven to 180°C (160°C fan-forced).

Place the fish in a bowl and add the curry paste, egg, rice flour, fish sauce, grated coconut and coconut milk. Mix gently until well combined, then add the kaffir lime leaves and holy basil and stir to combine.

Cut the banana leaves into 15 cm-wide strips and place 5 tablespoons of the fish mixture in the middle of a leaf strip. Fold up both sides and ends to make a parcel and secure with a short bamboo skewer or toothpick. Repeat with the remaining fish mixture and strips of banana leaf.

Place the banana leaf parcels on a baking tray or in a roasting tin and bake for 20–30 minutes or until the fish mixture is cooked. Serve.

PLA THARY TORD KAMIN
DEEP-FRIED RED-SPOT WHITING

SERVES 8 AS PART OF A SHARED MEAL

This was another of my favourite dishes when I lived in Phuket with my partner's family. Back then, the cook bought very small baby red-spot sand whiting and deep-fried them until they were crisp on the outside, while the white flesh remained soft and moist. When you gain more cooking experience, you can cook these little fish to the point where the heads are so crisp you can eat the whole fish. Fresh turmeric is the key to this dish, but if you can't find it you can use turmeric powder instead – just reduce the quantity to a teaspoon or two.

10 large cloves garlic, unpeeled
2–3 coriander roots, well washed
2 × 8 cm pieces fresh turmeric, chopped
1 large stick lemongrass, tender white
    part only, chopped
1 tablespoon black peppercorns, crushed
2 tablespoons light soy sauce

2 teaspoons Thai seasoning sauce
    (see page 195)
1 kg red-spot whiting, cleaned and scaled
vegetable oil, for deep-frying
Seafood Dipping Sauce (see page 191),
    to serve

Place the garlic, coriander roots, turmeric, lemongrass and peppercorns in a mortar and use the pestle to pound to a coarse paste (or blend in a blender). Transfer the mixture to a large bowl and add the light soy sauce and seasoning sauce, then stir to combine. Add the whiting and turn gently to coat. Cover with plastic film and marinate in the fridge for 30 minutes for the flavours to develop.

Heat vegetable oil for deep-frying in a deep-fryer or large heavy-based saucepan until it registers 160°C on a sugar/deep-fry thermometer. Working in batches, add a few whiting at a time, taking care as the mixture will spit. Deep-fry the fish for 5–8 minutes or until they are just cooked through. Remove with a slotted spoon and drain on paper towel. Repeat with the remaining fish.

Serve the fish with the seafood dipping sauce alongside.

PLA LARD PHRIK

DEEP-FRIED SNAPPER WITH HOMEMADE CURRY SAUCE

SERVES 6 AS PART OF A SHARED MEAL

Pla lard phrik is a thick style of curry where the red curry paste (see page 184) base is cooked with oil first before seasoning with palm sugar and fish sauce only. Coconut cream is not used in this dish, so if you want to make it more saucy you may need to add a little stock or water instead. Kaffir lime leaf is a must to add at the end here – it is the ingredient that brings this dish to life.

700 g snapper fillets, skin on and pin-boned
   (or 1 × 600 g snapper, cleaned
   and scaled)
50 g tapioca flour (see page 195)
vegetable oil, for deep-frying
3 kaffir lime leaves, torn

CURRY SAUCE
100 ml vegetable oil
200 g Red Curry Paste (see page 184)
⅓ cup (80 ml) fish sauce
⅓ cup (120 g) soft palm sugar
50 ml water
3 kaffir lime leaves, julienned
3 large fresh red chillies, thinly sliced
   on the diagonal

Dust the snapper with tapioca flour and shake off any excess.

Heat vegetable oil for deep-frying in a deep-fryer or large heavy-based saucepan until it reaches 180°C on a sugar/deep-fry thermometer. Deep-fry the snapper for 8 minutes or until golden and cooked through. Remove with a slotted spoon or tongs and drain on paper towel.

For the curry sauce, heat the vegetable oil in a heavy-based saucepan over medium heat. Add the curry paste, then stir for 2–3 minutes until aromatic. Add the fish sauce, palm sugar and water and stir until the sugar has dissolved. Place the kaffir lime leaves and half of the chilli in the pan and stir to combine.

Place the snapper on a plate or shallow serving dish and pour the curry sauce over. Scatter the torn kaffir lime leaves over the fish, along with the remaining chilli, if desired, then serve.

PLA NUENG TAO JIEW

STEAMED KINGFISH FILLET WITH SOYBEAN PASTE

SERVES 4 AS PART OF A SHARED MEAL

This super-lean dish involves a combination of Thai and Chinese cooking methods. The amount of hot chilli may be adjusted to suit your taste. The best fish to use here is kingfish, although coral trout cutlets are also excellent cooked this way. This dish produces a lot of liquid in the steamer, so it is best to use more, rather than less, seasoning to maintain strength of flavour.

6–7 large cloves garlic, finely chopped
1 × 4 cm piece ginger, finely chopped,
   plus 1 × 2 cm piece, julienned, for garnish
2 red birds-eye chillies, finely chopped
1 tablespoon soybean paste (see page 195)

3 teaspoons white sugar
50 ml water
500 g kingfish fillets, skin on and
   pin-boned, cut into 2 cm-thick slices
thinly sliced red birds-eye chilli, to serve

Place the garlic, chopped ginger and chilli, soybean paste, sugar and water in a bowl and stir until the sugar has dissolved.

Place the kingfish in a shallow heatproof bowl and spread with the garlic mixture.

Place a steamer basket over a saucepan of simmering water, then put the bowl of fish into the steamer. Cover and steam the fish over high heat for 10–12 minutes or until it is cooked through and tender.

Remove the fish and serve garnished with the julienned ginger and sliced chilli, with a little of the cooking broth spooned around.

GAI YANG
ROASTED MARINATED CHICKEN

SERVES 10 AS PART OF A SHARED MEAL

In the past, *gai yang* had only one marinating ingredient, which was homemade fish sauce, so the natural flavour came from the salt penetrating the flesh of the chicken. It was eaten with a chilli dipping sauce and sticky rice. Nowadays, this simple dish has developed to include loads of herbs and spices in the marinade resulting in delicious, crispy skin. Traditionally, the chicken is cooked over a charcoal barbecue, but here I've adapted it to roasting in the oven so there are no excuses not to try this at home!

1 large stick lemongrass, tender white part only, finely chopped
3 red shallots, roughly chopped
2 coriander roots, well washed
1 tablespoon black peppercorns
10 large cloves garlic
¼ cup (60 ml) light soy sauce
¼ cup (60 ml) Thai seasoning sauce (see page 195)

¼ cup (60 ml) oyster sauce
¼ cup (60 ml) fish sauce
1 tablespoon soft palm sugar
100 ml vegetable oil
2 teaspoons ground turmeric
2 teaspoons ground coriander
2 × 1.2 kg chickens, butterflied
Sweet Chilli Sauce (see page 187), to serve

Place the lemongrass, shallot, coriander roots, black peppercorns and garlic in a mortar and pound to a coarse paste with the pestle (or blend in a blender). Transfer the mixture to a large glass or stainless-steel bowl and add the soy sauce, seasoning sauce, oyster sauce, fish sauce, palm sugar, vegetable oil, turmeric and coriander and stir until well combined. Add the chickens and turn to coat with the marinade. Cover with plastic film and leave to marinate in the fridge for at least 30 minutes (or up to 24 hours) for the flavours to develop.

Preheat the oven to 180°C (160°C fan-forced).

Transfer the chickens to a baking dish or roasting pan, skin-side up, and roast for 40–45 minutes or until browned and cooked through. Remove and rest, loosely covered with foil, for 10 minutes. Carve into pieces and serve with sweet chilli sauce.

TAO JIEW LOUN

PORK BRAISED WITH SOYBEAN PASTE

SERVES 6 AS PART OF A SHARED MEAL

This has to be one of the dishes we cook most often in my family. Whenever we get together, you can be guaranteed that this will be on the table for us to share, with a huge selection of crisp vegetables alongside, such as cucumber, raw apple eggplant, any variety of lettuce and wedges of Chinese cabbage. While my family prefers this quite hot, you can reduce the number of chillies, if you prefer things a little less spicy.

3 large red shallots, roughly chopped
150 g soybean paste (see page 195)
350 ml coconut milk
150 g lean minced pork
6 large fresh green chillies, thickly sliced
6 large fresh red chillies, thickly sliced
¾ stick lemongrass, very thinly sliced
1 × 40 g piece galangal (see page 194), sliced

2 tablespoons tamarind puree (see page 195)
2 tablespoons soft palm sugar
5 kaffir lime leaves, torn
selection of crisp vegetables (such as cucumber, lettuce, apple eggplants (aubergines), baby carrots and blanched baby corn), to serve

Place the shallot and soybean paste in a mortar and use the pestle to pound to a coarse paste.

Combine the coconut milk and pork in a heavy-based saucepan and add the shallot paste, then stir over medium heat to separate the pork and remove any lumps. Add the chilli, lemongrass, galangal, tamarind and palm sugar and stir gently for 5–8 minutes or until the pork is cooked through. Remove from the heat and stir in the kaffir lime leaves. Serve with crisp raw vegetables for dipping.

DESSERTS

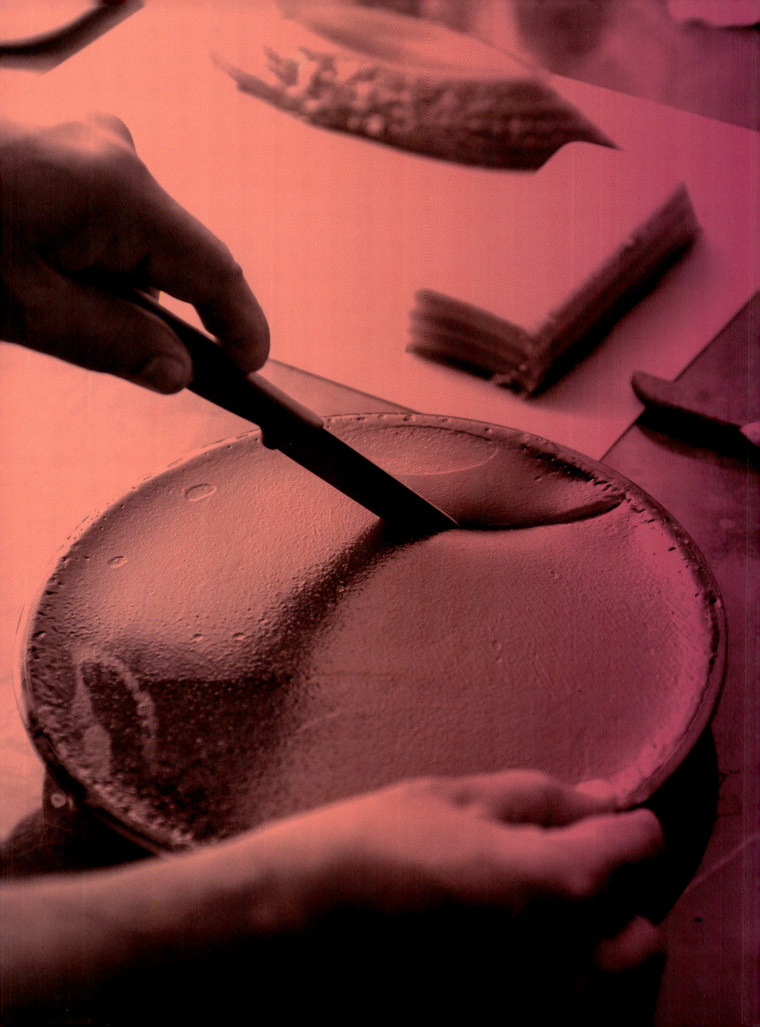

KHA NOM CHAN
STEAMED THAI LAYER CAKE

MAKES ABOUT 36 PIECES

This amazing dessert is common throughout Thailand. The colour is really interesting – and all natural! The richness of the coconut milk balances the sweetness from all the sugar.

300 g beetroot, roughly chopped
500 g white sugar
1.4 litres coconut milk

300 g tapioca flour (see page 195)
250 g arrowroot flour (available in the
    baking section of larger supermarkets)

Place the beetroot in a blender and blend for 1 minute. Spoon onto a clean muslin cloth, then squeeze the juice into a bowl. Discard the solids. Set the juice aside.

Place the sugar and 400 ml of the coconut milk in a heavy-based saucepan and stir over medium heat until the sugar has dissolved. Add the remaining coconut milk and stir well. Gradually add the tapioca flour and arrowroot, stirring after each addition until the mixture is smooth. Strain the coconut mixture through a muslin cloth into a heatproof jug or bowl, then divide evenly between 2 heatproof bowls. Add the beetroot juice to one of the bowls and stir until smooth.

Place a steamer basket over a saucepan of simmering water, then place a lightly greased 19 cm square cake tin inside the steamer. Pour 200 ml of the white coconut mixture into the tin and steam for 5 minutes or until firm. Carefully remove the cake tin from the steamer and pour 200 ml of the beetroot coconut mixture on top of the white coconut mixture. Return to the steamer and steam for 5 minutes or until firm. Repeat this layering process, using 200 ml of each liquid alternately and steaming for 5 minutes for each layer, finishing with the beetroot mixture as the final layer.

Leave the cake to cool completely. Cut into approximately 3 cm squares or diamonds. The cake can be stored in an airtight container at room temperature for up to 2 days; do not refrigerate.

KHA NOM KLOUY
STEAMED THAI BANANA CAKE

SERVES 6-8

In Thailand, this dessert is equally popular with both young and old people – it is easy to make, nutritious and the ingredients are inexpensive. In Australia, you may need to visit an Asian food store to get the grated frozen coconut, and the sugar bananas are usually more expensive than regular bananas. A touch of salt enhances the sweet flavour.

520 g (about 3–4) ripe lady finger
   bananas (sugar bananas)
200 ml coconut cream
150 g white sugar

1 teaspoon salt
60 g rice flour
200 g frozen grated coconut
   (see page 194), thawed

Coarsely mash the bananas in a bowl. Add the coconut cream, sugar, salt, rice flour and 120 g of the grated coconut and mix well.

Spoon the mixture into a 20 cm-diameter, 6 cm-deep, round baking dish and sprinkle over the remaining grated coconut. Place the dish in a large steamer basket and steam over a pan of simmering water for 35 minutes or until a skewer inserted in the centre comes out clean.

Leave to cool completely. Cut into slices and serve. The cake can be stored in an airtight container at room temperature for up to 2 days or in the fridge for up to 1 week.

KHA NOM TAOUY
STEAMED RICE PUDDINGS

MAKES 12

The base of this simple sweet consists only of rice flour, palm sugar and coconut cream, yet I think it is one of the best traditional Thai desserts there is. Be aware that the different fat content in different brands of coconut cream can affect the look of the pudding. You need to cook this over high heat to ensure the tops of the puddings are cooked.

50 g rice flour
70 g soft palm sugar
1 cup (250 ml) coconut cream

TOPPING
30 g rice flour
1 cup (250 ml) coconut cream
50 g white sugar
1 teaspoon salt

Place the rice flour, palm sugar and coconut cream in a bowl and mix until smooth and combined. Strain the mixture through a muslin cloth and divide evenly among twelve ¼-cup (60 ml-capacity) heatproof bowls.

Place a large steamer basket over a saucepan of simmering water. Place the bowls in the steamer and steam the puddings over high heat for 10–12 minutes or until just set.

Meanwhile, for the topping, place the rice flour, coconut cream, sugar and salt in a bowl and stir until the sugar has dissolved. Divide the topping mixture evenly among the puddings and steam for a further 10–12 minutes or until the topping has set.

Remove the puddings and leave to cool to room temperature, then serve. (The puddings can be covered with plastic film and stored at room temperature for up to 1 day, in the fridge for up to 1 week, or frozen for up to 1 month. Reheat in a steamer basket over a pan of simmering water for 5 minutes or until warm before serving.)

KHA NOM TOUA PAEB
MUNG BEAN & COCONUT DUMPLINGS

MAKES 12–14

Rice flour, plus different forms of sugar and coconut are the key ingredients in Thai desserts. When I was a child, my mother never bought processed rice flour, she made it herself. Here, it is combined with unprocessed coconut flesh, mung beans and sesame seeds to make a lovely dessert.

100 g yellow mung beans (see page 195)
1 teaspoon salt
75 g frozen grated coconut (see page 194), thawed
200 g glutinous rice flour (see page 194)
¾ cup (180 ml) boiling water

TOPPING
25 g white sesame seeds, toasted
25 g black sesame seeds, toasted
25 g caster sugar

Place the mung beans in a bowl, cover with cold water and leave to soak for 1 hour. Drain the mung beans, then place in a heatproof bowl in a steamer basket over a saucepan of simmering water and steam for 30 minutes. Leave to cool to room temperature.

Transfer half of the mung beans to a small bowl. Spread the remaining mung beans over a plate and combine with the salt and grated coconut for the coating.

Place the glutinous rice flour in a bowl, add ¼ cup (60 ml) of the boiling water and stir well, then add another ¼ cup (60 ml) of the boiling water and stir. Add the remaining boiling water and stir well. Knead the mixture to a soft dough, then cover with a damp tea towel.

Working in batches, take a small amount of the dough and, using floured hands, roll into a 3 cm diameter ball. Flatten the ball to a 6 cm disc, then place a teaspoonful of the steamed mung beans in the centre. Bring the dough up over the mung beans to enclose the filling, pinching to seal and form a flat oval parcel. Repeat with the remaining dough and mung beans to make 12–14 parcels.

Place the mung bean dumplings in a steamer basket over a saucepan of simmering water, then steam for 15 minutes or until cooked and tender. Remove the dumplings from the steamer and, while still warm, roll gently in the grated coconut mixture to coat.

For the topping, place the white and black sesame seeds in a mortar and use the pestle to lightly crush, then mix in the caster sugar.

To serve, dust the dumplings with the sesame sugar topping. The dumplings are best eaten on the day of making. They can be stored in an airtight container at room temperature for up to 1 day; do not refrigerate.

KHAO NIEW TAD
STEAMED STICKY RICE CAKE

SERVES 6–8

This interesting dessert uses whole grains of sticky rice, rather than rice flour. It is best made with the palest and longest-grained glutinous white rice available. The black-bean topping must be cooked using as high a heat as possible to ensure it sets. You will need to soak the glutinous rice for 12 hours before cooking.

250 g glutinous white rice
200 ml coconut milk
1 teaspoon salt
50 g white sugar

BLACK-BEAN TOPPING
200 g tinned black beans in brine
   (available from Asian food stores),
   rinsed and drained
150 ml coconut milk
2 tablespoons rice flour
100 g white sugar
1 teaspoon salt

Soak the glutinous rice in a bowl of water for 12 hours. Drain.

Spoon the rice into a 12 cm × 7 cm × 6 cm baking dish. Place the coconut milk, salt and sugar in a small bowl, then stir well to combine and pour over the rice.

Place the baking dish in a large steamer basket over a large saucepan of simmering water and steam over high heat for 30 minutes.

For the topping, spoon the black beans over the cooked rice mixture. Place the coconut milk, rice flour, sugar and salt in a bowl and stir to combine, then pour over the black beans. Steam over high heat for another 15 minutes.

Remove and leave to cool to room temperature. Cut into square pieces and serve. The cake can be stored in an airtight container for up to 2 days at room temperature, or up to 1 week in the fridge. Reheat in a steamer basket over a saucepan of simmering water or microwave to warm through before serving.

MOR KAENG TUA
MUNG BEAN CAKE

MAKES ABOUT 10 PIECES

This is the only dessert in this cookbook that contains no rice-based component; instead it is based on mung beans and eggs. It shows how Thai cooking has adapted to include the Western use of eggs in desserts, in tandem with the more traditional palm sugar, coconut milk and savoury touch of fried shallots. The mung beans need to be soaked for 1 hour before cooking.

100 g yellow mung beans (see page 195)
200 ml coconut milk
150 g soft palm sugar

3 eggs, lightly beaten
¼ cup (20 g) Fried Red Shallots
  (see page 179)

Place the mung beans in a bowl, cover with hot water and leave to soak for 1 hour.

Drain the mung beans, then place in a heatproof bowl in a steamer basket over a saucepan of simmering water and steam for 25–30 minutes or until tender. Leave to cool to room temperature.

Preheat the oven to 160°C (140°C fan-forced).

Place the coconut milk, three-quarters of the mung beans, the palm sugar and egg in a blender or food processor and pulse briefly until the sugar has dissolved. Transfer the mixture to a heavy-based saucepan and add the remaining mung beans, then cover and cook over low heat for 2–3 minutes, stirring frequently.

Pour the bean mixture into a 15 cm × 8 cm × 5 cm baking dish and bake for 40–45 minutes or until just firm in the centre. Leave to cool to room temperature.

Sprinkle with the shallots and cut into 4 cm × 3 cm pieces, then serve. The mung bean cake can be stored in an airtight container for up to 2 days at room temperature or in the fridge for up to 1 week. Reheat in a 160°C oven to warm through before serving.

THAI KITCHEN ESSENTIALS

MOO KROB
CRISPY PORK BELLY
MAKES 1 KG

1 × 1 kg piece boneless pork belly
1 tablespoon salt
5 litres water, as needed
2 litres vegetable oil

Place the pork belly, salt and enough water to cover the pork in a large stockpot and bring to the boil over medium heat. Reduce the heat to low and simmer, covered, for 1½ hours. Drain the pork and place in a baking dish or bowl in the fridge for 30 minutes.

Slice the chilled pork into 2 cm-wide strips and pat dry with paper towel.

Heat the vegetable oil in a large, deep, heavy-based saucepan over medium heat. When hot, add half of the pork, covering the pan immediately as the hot oil will spit. Watch carefully, then when the bubbling in the oil subsides, remove the lid and cook the pork for a further 5–6 minutes, stirring occasionally, until it is brown and cooked through. Remove with a slotted spoon or wire strainer and drain on paper towel. Repeat with the remaining pork belly pieces. Set aside to cool.

Transfer the pork to an airtight container and store in the fridge for up to 2 days. (See picture on page 175).

NUA TUAN
SLOW-COOKED BEEF
MAKES 1 KG

1 kg chuck steak, cut into 6 cm pieces
1 tablespoon salt
4 litres water, as needed
1 stick lemongrass, cut into 8 cm length,
   leaf section tied in a knot

Place the beef, salt and enough water to cover in a large heavy-based saucepan and bring to the boil over medium heat, stirring occasionally and skimming the surface of impurities as necessary. Reduce the heat to low, add the lemongrass and simmer for 1½ hours. Remove from the heat and set the beef aside to cool in the liquid for 2 hours, then drain the beef well, discarding the liquid and lemongrass.

Transfer the beef to an airtight container and refrigerate until using; this is best used on the day it is made.

KHAO KUA
GROUND ROASTED RICE
MAKES ABOUT 1½ CUPS

300 g glutinous white rice
1 × 20 g piece galangal (see page 194), finely chopped
½ stick lemongrass, sliced
5 kaffir lime leaves

Place the rice, galangal, lemongrass and kaffir lime leaves in a heavy-based frying pan over low heat. Cook, stirring constantly so the rice doesn't burn, for 6–8 minutes or until the rice is pale golden. Remove from the heat and discard the galangal, lemongrass and kaffir lime leaves. Leave the rice to cool to room temperature.

Place the rice in a mortar and finely grind with the pestle (or use a small food processor or spice grinder).

Store in an airtight container in a cool, dry place for up to 2 weeks.

NAM POON SAI
LIME WATER
MAKES ABOUT 1 LITRE

1 tablespoon lime paste (see page 194)
1 litre water

Combine the lime paste and water in a large bowl and stir to dissolve, then set aside for 30 minutes. It is ready to use when the pink paste has settled in the bottom of the water – you only use the clear liquid on top and discard the rest.

Store in a sterilised glass bottle in the fridge for up to 1 week and use in recipes as specified.

KRA TEIAM JEAW
FRIED GARLIC
MAKES ABOUT 300 G

2 cups (500 ml) vegetable oil
300 g cloves garlic (about 4–5 bulbs), chopped

Heat the oil in a wok or deep heavy-based saucepan over high heat until it reaches 160°C on a sugar/deep-fry thermometer, then add the garlic and stir for 4–5 minutes, ensuring the garlic doesn't burn. Remove the garlic from the oil with a slotted spoon or wire basket and drain on paper towel; discard the oil.

   Transfer to an airtight container and store in a cool, dry place for up to 2 weeks.

HOM JEAW
FRIED RED SHALLOTS
MAKES ABOUT 300 G

2 cups (500 ml) vegetable oil
300 g (about 12) red shallots, thinly sliced

Heat the oil in a wok or deep heavy-based saucepan over high heat until it reaches 160°C on a sugar/deep-fry thermometer. Add the shallot and stir for 4–5 minutes, ensuring the shallot doesn't burn. Remove the shallot from the oil with a slotted spoon or wire basket and drain on paper towel; discard the oil.

   Transfer to an airtight container and store in a cool, dry place for up to 2 weeks.

KREUNG GAENG DANG PED
RED DUCK CURRY PASTE

MAKES ABOUT 400 G

10 g small dried red chillies
30 g large dried red chillies
5 cloves garlic, peeled
½ stick lemongrass, sliced
1 large red shallot, sliced
1 × 30 g piece galangal (see page 194),
    peeled and roughly chopped
1 × 10 g piece fresh turmeric, peeled and sliced
50 g shrimp paste
20 g kaffir lime rind
½ teaspoon ground cloves
½ teaspoon ground nutmeg
200 ml water

Place the small and large dried chillies in a bowl of warm water and set aside for 3–4 minutes, then drain.

Combine the drained chillies, garlic, lemongrass, shallot, galangal, turmeric, shrimp paste, lime rind, cloves, nutmeg and water in a blender and blend to a smooth paste.

Store in an airtight container in the fridge for 3–5 days or freezer for up to 2 months.

KREUNG GAENG KEOW WANN
GREEN CURRY PASTE

MAKES ABOUT 500 G

80 g fresh long green chillies, stems removed
    and roughly chopped
50 g fresh small green chillies, stems removed
5 cloves garlic, peeled
½ stick lemongrass, thinly sliced
1 red shallot, sliced
1 × 20 g piece galangal (see page 194), peeled
    and roughly chopped
1 × 10 g piece fresh turmeric, peeled and sliced
30 g shrimp paste
20 g kaffir lime rind
1 teaspoon ground coriander
1 teaspoon ground cumin
200 ml water

Place the chillies, garlic, lemongrass, shallot, galangal, turmeric, shrimp paste, lime rind, spices and water in a blender and blend to a smooth paste.

Store in an airtight container in the fridge for 3–5 days or freezer for up to 2 months.

KREUNG GAENG MASSAMAN
MASSAMAN CURRY PASTE

MAKES ABOUT 4 CUPS (800 G)

2 cups (500 ml) vegetable oil, plus extra
    for sealing
30 g small dried red chillies
100 g large dried chillies
8 red shallots, sliced
20 cloves garlic, sliced
1 × 200 g piece fresh ginger, peeled and sliced
3 teaspoons ground cloves
3 teaspoons ground cumin
3 teaspoons ground aniseed
1½ teaspoons ground star anise
3 teaspoons ground cinnamon
3 teaspoons ground nutmeg
1 teaspoon ground turmeric

Heat the vegetable oil in a very large heavy-based saucepan over low heat. Add the chillies, shallot, garlic, ginger and spices and stir for 7–10 minutes until aromatic, then remove from the heat.

Leave to cool slightly and then, working in batches, transfer the chilli and spice mixture to a blender and blend to a smooth paste. Transfer the curry paste to an airtight container and cover with a film of vegetable oil, then store in the fridge for 3–5 days or freezer for up to 3 months.

RED DUCK CURRY PASTE

MASSAMAN CURRY PASTE

GREEN CURRY PASTE

SOUR CURRY PASTE

YELLOW CURRY PASTE

PANANG CURRY PASTE

KREUNG GAENG SOM
SOUR CURRY PASTE
MAKES ABOUT 520 G

1 × 120 g white fish fillet (such as flathead
   or snapper), skin removed and pin-boned
1 cup (250 ml) water
30 g large dried red chillies
10 g small dried red chillies
2 cloves garlic, peeled
¼ stick lemongrass, sliced
4 red shallots, sliced
60 g shrimp paste
50 g krachai (see page 194), rinsed and
   drained if pickled in brine
30 g kaffir lime rind

Place the fish and water in a small heavy-based
saucepan and bring to the boil over medium
heat. Reduce the heat to low and simmer for
1–2 minutes until the fish is just cooked. Remove
the fish and drain, reserving the cooking liquid.

   Place the dried chillies in a bowl of warm water
and set aside for 3–4 minutes, then drain.

   Combine the drained chillies, garlic, lemongrass,
shallot, shrimp paste, krachai, lime rind, fish and
cooking liquid in a blender. Blend to a smooth paste.

   Store in an airtight container in the fridge for
2–3 days or freezer for up to 2 months.

KREUNG GAENG KA REE
YELLOW CURRY PASTE
MAKES ABOUT 380 G

20 g small dried red chillies
10 g large dried red chillies
4 cloves garlic, peeled
½ stick lemongrass, sliced
2 red shallots, sliced
1 × 40 g piece ginger, peeled and sliced
20 g shrimp paste
2 tablespoons medium curry powder
1 teaspoon ground turmeric
1 teaspoon ground coriander
1 teaspoon ground cumin
200 ml water

Place the dried chillies in a bowl of warm water
and set aside for 3–4 minutes, then drain.

   Combine the drained chillies, garlic, lemongrass,
shallot, ginger, shrimp paste, spices and water
in a blender. Blend to a smooth paste.

   Store in an airtight container in the fridge for
3–5 days or freezer for up to 2 months.

KREUNG GAENG PANAENG
PANANG CURRY PASTE
MAKES ABOUT 360 G

30 g large dried red chillies
10 g small dried red chillies
4 cloves garlic, peeled
½ stick lemongrass, sliced
2 red shallots, sliced
1 × 20 g piece galangal (see page 194),
   peeled and roughly chopped
50 g shrimp paste
20 g kaffir lime rind
2 teaspoons ground coriander
1 teaspoon ground cumin
200 ml water

Place the dried chillies in a bowl of warm water
and set aside for 3–4 minutes, then drain.

   Combine the drained chillies, garlic, lemongrass,
shallot, galangal, shrimp paste, kaffir lime rind,
spices and water in a blender. Blend to a smooth
paste.

   Store in an airtight container in the fridge for
3–5 days or freezer for up to 2 months.

KREUNG GAENG DANG
RED CURRY PASTE
MAKES ABOUT 340 G

10 g small dried red chillies
30 g large dried red chillies
4 cloves garlic, peeled
½ stick lemongrass, sliced
1 red shallot, sliced
30 g shrimp paste (see page 195)
30 g kaffir lime rind
200 ml water

Place the dried chillies in a bowl of warm water and set aside for 3–4 minutes, then drain.

Place the drained chillies, garlic, lemongrass, shallot, shrimp paste, kaffir lime rind and water in a blender. Blend to a smooth paste.

Store in an airtight container in the fridge for 3–5 days or freezer for up to 2 months.

KREUNG GAENG PAD CHA
PAD CHA CURRY PASTE
MAKES ABOUT 110 G

20 g red birds-eye chillies
20 g fresh long green chillies
5 cloves garlic, peeled
½ stick lemongrass, thinly sliced
1 small red shallot, sliced
1 × 25 g piece fresh turmeric, peeled and sliced
2 teaspoons black peppercorns

Place the chillies, garlic, lemongrass, shallot, turmeric and peppercorns in a mortar and pound with the pestle to form a coarse paste.

Store in an airtight container in the fridge for 3–5 days or freezer for up to 2 months.

KREUNG GAENG ISSAN
ISSAN CURRY PASTE
MAKES ABOUT 200 G

50 g red or green birds-eye chillies
10 cloves garlic, peeled
1 stick lemongrass, thinly sliced
3 red shallots, sliced

Place the chillies, garlic, lemongrass and shallot in a food processor and blend to a coarse paste.

Store in an airtight container for 3–5 days or freezer for up to 2 months.

PAD CHA CURRY PASTE

RED CURRY PASTE

ISSAN CURRY PASTE

KREUNG GAENG TAI
SOUTHERN CURRY PASTE
MAKES ABOUT 500 G

30 g small dried red chillies
25 g large dried red chillies
15 cloves garlic, peeled
1 × 30 g piece galangal (see page 194),
   peeled and roughly chopped
1 stick lemongrass, sliced
1 × 70 g piece fresh turmeric, peeled and sliced
3 red shallots, sliced
50 g shrimp paste (see page 195)
15 g kaffir lime rind
3 teaspoons black peppercorns
200 ml water

Place the dried chillies in a bowl of warm water and set aside for 3–4 minutes, then drain.

Place the drained chillies, garlic, galangal, lemongrass, turmeric, shallot, shrimp paste, kaffir lime rind, peppercorns and water in a blender. Blend to a smooth paste.

Store in an airtight container in the fridge for 3–5 days or freezer for up to 2 months.

KREUNG GAENG PA
JUNGLE CURRY PASTE
MAKES ABOUT 500 G

This recipe needs to be started 30 minutes ahead of using.

1 tablespoon long-grain rice
40 g small dried red chillies
30 g large dried red chillies
10 cloves garlic, peeled
1 × 50 g piece galangal (see page 194),
   peeled and roughly chopped
1 stick lemongrass, sliced
2 red shallots, sliced
50 g shrimp paste (see page 195)
30 g kaffir lime rind
3 teaspoons black peppercorns
200 ml water

Soak the rice in a small bowl of cold water for 30 minutes, then drain.

Place the dried chillies in a bowl of warm water and set aside for 3–4 minutes, then drain.

Place the drained rice, chillies, garlic, galangal, lemongrass, shallot, shrimp paste, kaffir lime rind, peppercorns and water in a blender. Blend to a smooth paste.

Store in an airtight container in the fridge for 3–5 days or freezer for up to 2 months.

NAM MA KHAM
TAMARIND SAUCE

MAKES ABOUT 2 CUPS (500 ML)

¼ cup (60 ml) vegetable oil
2 small dried chillies
3 large cloves garlic, chopped
3 large fresh red chillies, julienned
8 red shallots, sliced
3 red birds-eye chillies, chopped
¼ cup (60 ml) fish sauce
¼ cup (60 ml) tamarind puree (see page 195)
150 g soft palm sugar
1 teaspoon salt
200 ml water

Heat the oil in a deep heavy-based saucepan over high heat. Add the dried chillies, then deep-fry until crisp. Remove with tongs and drain on paper towel. Add the garlic and large fresh chilli to the pan and cook for 1 minute, then add the shallot and continue cooking for another 1 minute, then add the birds-eye chilli, fish sauce, tamarind, palm sugar and salt and stir until the sugar has dissolved.

Crumble the deep-fried dried chillies. Carefully add the water and dried chilli to the sauce, then simmer over medium heat for 5 minutes. Leave to cool to room temperature, then transfer to a bowl.

Leftover tamarind sauce can be stored in an airtight container in the fridge for up to 2 weeks.

NAM JIM SWEET CHILLI
SWEET CHILLI SAUCE

MAKES ABOUT 2½ CUPS (625ML)

12–15 large fresh red chillies, roughly chopped
2½ bulbs garlic (about 250 g), peeled
500 g white sugar
2 cups (500 ml) white vinegar
2 tablespoons salt

Place the chilli and garlic in a food processor and pulse until finely chopped. Transfer to a heavy-based saucepan and add the sugar, vinegar and salt. Cook the chilli sauce over medium heat for 3 minutes, stirring until the sugar has dissolved. Bring to the boil, then reduce the heat to low and simmer for 20–25 minutes, stirring occasionally, until the mixture is slightly reduced and thickened.

Leave to cool, then store in an airtight container in the fridge for up to 4 weeks.

Bring to room temperature before serving.

KAO NIOW
STEAMED STICKY RICE

SERVES 4 AS PART OF A SHARED MEAL

The rice needs to be soaked for at least one hour before cooking.

2 cups (400 g) glutinous white rice

Place the rice in a bowl, add enough cold or lukewarm water to cover it completely and soak for at least 1 hour or overnight if possible.

Drain the rice and place in a bamboo steamer basket lined with baking paper or muslin and steam over a saucepan of simmering water for 20 minutes or until the rice is translucent, soft and chewy.

NAM PRIK PAO
CHILLI JAM
MAKES ABOUT 1½ CUPS

48–50 (20 g) small dried red chillies
45–48 (80 g) large dried red chillies
6 large red shallots, roughly chopped
20 large cloves garlic, roughly chopped
1 cup (250 ml) vegetable oil
150 ml fish sauce
100 g tamarind puree (see page 195)
150 g soft palm sugar
100 g dried shrimp (see page 194), ground

Place the dried chillies in a bowl of warm water
and leave to soak for 3–4 minutes, then drain.

Place the drained chillies, shallot and garlic
in a dry heavy-based frying pan and stir over
medium heat until the garlic and shallot are
tender. Transfer to a food processor and process
to form a coarse paste.

Heat the oil in a heavy-based frying pan over
low heat and add the chilli mixture, then stir for
4–5 minutes. Add the fish sauce, tamarind puree
and palm sugar and stir until the mixture comes
to the boil. Reduce the heat and simmer for
3–4 minutes, then add the ground shrimp,
stir well to combine and remove from the heat.

Store in an airtight container in the fridge
for up to 1 month.

NAM JIM SATAY
PEANUT SAUCE
MAKES ABOUT 4 CUPS

150 ml vegetable oil
100 g Red Curry Paste (see page 184)
2 cups (500 ml) coconut milk
5 star anise
1 stick cinnamon
1 teaspoon ground cinnamon
3½ tablespoons (100 g) soft palm sugar
2 teaspoons salt
¼ cup (60 ml) tamarind puree (see page 195)
1⅔ cups (250 g) roasted unsalted
   peanuts, coarsely ground

Place the vegetable oil and curry paste in a small
heavy-based saucepan and stir over low heat for
2–3 minutes until aromatic. Add the coconut milk,
spices, palm sugar, salt and tamarind puree and
stir gently until boiling. Remove from the heat and
leave to cool. Remove the star anise and cinnamon
stick, then add the peanuts and stir to mix well.
Transfer to a bowl.

Leftovers can be stored in an airtight container
in the fridge for up to 4 days. Alternatively, you
can halve the ingredients to make 2 cups.

NAM JIM JAEW MA KHUA TAET
TOMATO *JIM JAEW* DIPPING SAUCE
MAKES ABOUT 1 CUP

9 cherry tomatoes
6 large fresh red chillies
1 small red shallot, peeled
5 large cloves garlic, peeled
3 teaspoons fermented fish sauce (see page 194)
3 teaspoons fish sauce

Place the tomatoes, chillies, shallot and garlic in
a dry heavy-based frying pan and dry-roast over
medium heat, shaking the pan often, until the
vegetables are tender. Peel and discard the skin
from the chillies, then transfer the flesh to a food
processor with the shallot, garlic and tomatoes.
Pulse briefly, add the fish sauces and pulse
to combine, then transfer to a bowl.

CHILLI JAM

PEANUT SAUCE

TOMATO *JIM JAEW* DIPPING SAUCE

SEASONING VINEGAR

TAMARIND
JIM JAEW DIPPING SAUCE

SEAFOOD DIPPING SAUCE

NAM SOM
SEASONING VINEGAR
MAKES ABOUT ½ CUP (125 ML)

6 large cloves garlic, peeled
8–9 red or green birds-eye chillies
3 teaspoons salt
2 teaspoons white sugar
100 ml white vinegar

Place the garlic and chillies in a dry heavy-based frying pan and cook over medium heat for 3–4 minutes until the garlic is soft. Transfer the garlic mixture to a mortar, then add the salt and sugar and pound with the pestle until smooth. Add the vinegar and stir well, then transfer to a bowl.

(This is often placed on the table to be used by those who prefer a more highly spiced meal. Leftovers can be stored in an airtight container in the fridge for up to 1 month.)

NAM JIM (FOR SEAFOOD)
SEAFOOD DIPPING SAUCE
MAKES ABOUT ⅔ CUP (160 ML)

2 large cloves garlic, peeled
1 small red shallot, peeled
3 small fresh green chillies, crushed
1–2 coriander roots, well washed
1½ tablespoons soft palm sugar
¼ cup (60 ml) fish sauce
⅓ cup (80 ml) lime juice
5–6 sprigs coriander, roughly chopped

Place the garlic, shallot, chillies and coriander roots in a mortar and pound with the pestle to form a coarse paste (or pulse in a food processor).

Transfer the paste to a bowl and add the palm sugar, fish sauce and lime juice, then stir until the sugar has dissolved. Taste the sauce – it should be a balance of sweet, sour and salty, so adjust if necessary. Garnish with chopped coriander leaves.

This sauce is ideal served with barbecued seafood and freshly shucked oysters.

NAM JIM JAEW MA KHAM PIEK
TAMARIND *JIM JAEW* DIPPING SAUCE
MAKES ABOUT 1 CUP (250 ML)

90 g tamarind puree (see page 195)
2½ tablespoons soft palm sugar
2½ tablespoons fish sauce
¼ cup (60 ml) hot water
3 teaspoons Ground Roasted Rice (see page 178)
1–2 teaspoons chilli powder, to taste

Place the tamarind puree, palm sugar, fish sauce and hot water in a small heavy-based saucepan, then, stirring constantly, bring to the boil over low heat. Remove from the heat and leave to cool to room temperature, then add the ground rice and chilli powder to taste and stir to mix well.

This sauce is ideal with grilled meat, particularly the chargrilled marinated pork skewers on page 18.

NAM YUM NUNAM JIM JAEW PRIK PON
ISSAN BARBECUE SAUCE
MAKES ABOUT ¾ CUP (180 ML)

100 ml fish sauce
1½ tablespoons lime juice
1 teaspoon white sugar
¼ cup (60 ml) boiling water
1 tablespoon Ground Roasted Rice (see page 178)
1 teaspoon chilli powder
5 cherry tomatoes, halved
3 kaffir lime leaves, finely chopped
6–7 leaves Vietnamese coriander (see page 195), roughly chopped

Combine the fish sauce, lime juice, sugar and boiling water in a bowl and stir until the sugar has dissolved. Add the ground roasted rice and chilli powder. Squeeze the tomatoes to release their seeds and flesh and add to the bowl with the kaffir lime leaves and Vietnamese coriander; discard the tomato skins. Stir to mix well, then transfer to a bowl.

This sauce is delicious served with barbecued meat and ox tongue.

NAM AJARD
CUCUMBER RELISH
MAKES ABOUT 1 CUP

100 ml white vinegar
100 g white sugar
1 teaspoon salt
1 lebanese cucumber, finely diced or halved lengthways and thinly sliced
2 large fresh red chillies, cut into 2 mm-thick slices
1 red shallot, thinly sliced
5–6 sprigs coriander

Place the vinegar, sugar and salt in a small heavy-based saucepan and stir over medium heat until the sugar has dissolved. Bring to the boil, then remove from the heat and leave to cool to room temperature.

Transfer the sauce to a bowl. Add the cucumber, chilli and shallot and stir well. Just before serving, garnish with coriander leaves.

NAM YUM NUA
BEEF SALAD DRESSING
MAKES ABOUT ⅔ CUP (160 ML)

3 green birds-eye chillies
6 large cloves garlic, peeled
3 coriander roots, well washed
1 tablespoon soft palm sugar
¼ cup (60 ml) fish sauce
3½ tablespoons lime juice

Place the chillies, garlic and coriander roots in a mortar and pound with a pestle until well combined to form a paste (or pulse in a food processor).

Transfer the paste to a bowl and add the palm sugar, fish sauce and lime juice and stir until the sugar has dissolved. Taste the sauce – it should be a balance of sweet, sour and salty, so adjust with a little more palm sugar, fish sauce or lime juice, if necessary.

ISSAN BARBECUE SAUCE

CUCUMBER RELISH

GLOSSARY

APPLE EGGPLANT (AUBERGINE)
This small, round, green eggplant (aubergine) takes its name from its similar appearance to Granny Smith apples. It is often added to Thai curries and, when cooked, has a mild flavour and creamy texture. Available from Asian and specialty greengrocers.

BANANA CHILLI/PEPPER
Also known as wax pepper chillies, these large, mild, pale-green chillies are used as a vegetable in stir-fries or for stuffing.

BIRDS-EYE CHILLI
These small red or green chillies are the spiciest variety and are used extensively in Thai cuisine.

CHINESE CELERY
The Chinese counterpart to common celery has thinner, longer, hollow stems and a more delicate flavour. Available from Asian greengrocers.

DRIED SHRIMP
These tiny, salted dried shrimp are available in packets from Asian food stores. They add protein and a salty, briny fish flavour and textural contrast to many Thai dishes.

FERMENTED FISH SAUCE
A more pungent version of regular Thai fish sauce (nam pla), this is commonly used in the Issan-style regional cooking of north-eastern Thailand. It is the liquid that results from combining fish, salt and rice bran in large barrels, then leaving the mixture to ferment for anywhere between three months and one year. Available from Asian food stores.

FROZEN GRATED COCONUT
The flesh of young coconuts that has been grated and frozen for use in curries, desserts and other dishes. Unlike dried shredded or flaked coconut, it retains the moist fleshiness of fresh coconut flesh. Available in packets in the freezer section of Asian food stores.

GALANGAL
This rhizome (root) is related to ginger is used in many Thai curry pastes and soups for its stronger ginger-like flavour and aroma.

GLUTINOUS RICE FLOUR
This fine flour is made by grinding glutinous or sticky rice. Despite its name, as it is rice-based, it contains no gluten; rather, this refers to its sticky quality when cooked in Thai sweets.

HOLY BASIL
The leaves of this aromatic herb have a reddish tip and the scent of cloves. They are used in many Thai stir-fries to add a fresh, herbaceous flavour just before serving. Available from Asian greengrocers.

KAFFIR LIME LEAF
The fragrant leaves of the kaffir lime tree are widely used in soups and curries, either cooked whole or thinly sliced and added before serving to give a fresh, citrusy note.

KRACHAI
Sometimes called fingerroot, grachai, lesser galangal or wild ginger, this rhizome is related to ginger. It has a slightly medicinal flavour and is commonly used in Thai fish and curry dishes.

LEMON BASIL
The fragrant leaves and seeds of this herb are used in some Thai curries and desserts to add a refreshing, citrusy note. Available from Asian greengrocers.

LIME PASTE
Contrary to its name, this paste is not made from the citrus fruit lime, but from red cockleshells that have been baked at a very high temperature, then made into a paste. This unslaked lime is then mixed with water to form an edible paste used in Thai cooking, often to add extra crispiness to deep-fried food. Available in containers from Asian food stores.

LONG MELON
This elongated, pale, tropical vegetable has a waxy coating that means it can be stored for long periods after picking, but the coating is easily removed before cooking, usually in curries or soups. It is appreciated in Thai cuisine for the interesting texture it adds to dishes it is cooked in. Available from Asian greengrocers, when in season in the colder months.

NOODLES – DRY AND FRESH

In recipes calling for rice noodles, you can use imported dry rice noodles or locally made fresh ones. The fresh noodles can be cooked straight from the packet in stir-fries, or blanched before adding to soups. Dry noodles need to be soaked in cold water until they soften, then drained well before using.

PANDAN LEAVES

Sometimes called screwpine, this sweet-smelling leaf is used for flavouring, colouring and wrapping other ingredients before cooking.

PEA EGGPLANT (AUBERGINE)

These tiny, pea-sized eggplants (aubergines) are added whole to Thai curries and soups. When cooked, they add texture as well as flavour, bursting in your mouth as you bite them, and releasing a sharp hint of bitterness.

ROUNDLEAF MINT

Used in Thai salads and cooked with some freshwater fish to minimise their muddy taste.

SHRIMP PASTE

This paste is made from fermented ground shrimp mixed with salt, and has a pungent aroma. Available from Asian food stores and some larger supermarkets.

SOYBEAN PASTE

Made from fermented and crushed soybeans, wheat flour, salt and water blended into paste form. Premium-quality brands use a natural fermentation process to produce the paste.

TAMARIND PUREE

The pureed form of the pulp of the tamarind pod is sold in jars and plastic containers in the Asian section of larger supermarkets, as well as Asian food stores. It is used to add its distinctive tart, yet smooth flavour, providing many Thai dishes with the sour element that is so important in Thai cuisine.

TAPIOCA FLOUR

Sometimes sold labelled as 'tapioca starch', this gluten-free flour is derived from dried tapioca (cassava) root, and is used as a thickener.

THAI SALTED CABBAGE

Sold in tins or jars in Asian food stores, this fermented Chinese cabbage (wombok) adds a complex, salty flavour to dishes it is used in.

THAI SEASONING SAUCE

Used extensively in Thai cooking. In Australia, Golden Mountain is one of the better-known brands of this important fermented soybean-based sauce. It is a little saltier and sweeter than soy sauce and contains wheat, so is not suitable for anyone following a gluten-free diet.

THAI SWEET BASIL

Used frequently in Thai cuisine, this Thai variety of basil features a mild, slightly aniseed taste. Available from Asian greengrocers.

VIETNAMESE CORIANDER

Also known as eryngo and saw-tooth coriander, this herb is used in north-eastern soups and curries that don't contain coconut milk.

YELLOW MUNG BEANS

These dried small legumes are used in Thai sweets, while the flour is used in some doughs and to make bean thread vermicelli.

YELLOW SOYBEAN PASTE

Available in jars from Asian food stores, this sweet and salty paste tastes stronger than soy sauce.

THANK YOU

There are many people who have helped bring this book to life.

Firstly, I must thank my parents, grandparents and mother-in-law, all of whom have spent much time guiding me and teaching me their cooking techniques and special recipes. Without them, this book would not have been written.

Thanks also to the team at Penguin, especially my publisher Julie Gibbs, publishing manager Katrina O'Brien, editor Kathleen Gandy, and production controller Tracey Jarrett, for their editing, patience and assistance during the long process of preparing this book.

Thanks also to talented designer Daniel New, photographer Rob Palmer and stylist Vanessa Austin, for creating such an outstanding design and visual look. Thanks, too, to Lynne Mullins for her assistance and guidance in the early stages of the book.

To Padet Nagsalab, my right hand – I can never thank you enough for your dedication, creativity, hard work and friendship.

To Suvimon Chaithavornkul, my main chef, thanks for your hard work, time and effort in preparing the Thai recipes.

To Lyle Wilson, special thanks for your many hours of tireless work and attention to detail behind the scenes to keep everything on track.

To Deirdre O'Loghlin of O'Loghlin Communications, a huge thanks for encouraging and supporting the team in making all of this come to fruition.

Last, but not least, I would like to thank all the staff in my restaurants, who help me daily in supplying and serving lovingly cooked fine Thai food.

INDEX

LANTERN

Published by the Penguin Group
Penguin Group (Australia)
707 Collins Street, Melbourne, Victoria 3008, Australia
(a division of Penguin Australia Pty Ltd)
Penguin Group (USA) Inc.
375 Hudson Street, New York, New York 10014, USA
Penguin Group (Canada)
90 Eglinton Avenue East, Suite 700, Toronto, Canada ON M4P 2Y3
(a division of Penguin Canada Books Inc.)
Penguin Books Ltd
80 Strand, London WC2R 0RL England
Penguin Ireland
25 St Stephen's Green, Dublin 2, Ireland
(a division of Penguin Books Ltd)
Penguin Books India Pvt Ltd
11 Community Centre, Panchsheel Park, New Delhi – 110 017, India
Penguin Group (NZ)
67 Apollo Drive, Rosedale, Auckland 0632, New Zealand
(a division of Penguin New Zealand Pty Ltd)
Penguin Books (South Africa) (Pty) Ltd, Rosebank Office Park, Block D,
181 Jan Smuts Avenue, Parktown North, Johannesburg, 2196, South Africa
Penguin (Beijing) Ltd
7F, Tower B, Jiaming Center, 27 East Third Ring Road North,
Chaoyang District, Beijing 100020, China

Penguin Books Ltd, Registered Offices: 80 Strand, London, WC2R 0RL, England

First published by Penguin Group (Australia), 2015

10 9 8 7 6 5 4 3 2 1

Design by Daniel New © Penguin Group (Australia)
Photography by Rob Palmer
Styling by Vanessa Austin
Typeset by Post Pre-Press Group, Brisbane, Queensland
Colour separation by Splitting Image Colour Studio, Clayton, Victoria
Printed and bound in China by 1010 Printing International Limited

National Library of Australia
Cataloguing-in-Publication data:

Saenkham, Sujet author.
Spice I Am : Homestyle Thai recipes / Sujet Saenkham ; Rob Palmer.
9781921383595 (paperback)
Includes index.
Cooking, Thai.
Palmer, Rob, photographer.

641.59593

penguin.com.au/lantern